Muffin Tin Chef

*101 Savory Snacks, Adorable Appetizers,
Enticing Entrees & Delicious Desserts*

|MATT KADEY|

MJF BOOKS
New York

Published by MJF Books
Fine Communications
322 Eighth Avenue
New York, NY 10001

Muffin Tin Chef
LC Control Number: 2012947626
ISBN-13: 978-1-60671-165-1
ISBN-10: 1-60671-165-2

This edition is published by MJF Books in arrangement with Ulysses Press
(www.ulyssespress.com).

Printed in China.

OGI   10   9   8   7   6   5   4   3   2

TABLE OF CONTENTS

INTRODUCTION
The Muffin Pan Can

So how does a male dietitian come to write a cookbook devoted to muffin tins? Well, it started with a magazine assignment I was given a few years ago to develop several recipes using the trusty muffin tin with one big stipulation: no muffins! At that point, muffins were all I had ever used one for. However, as I started to research recipes, I quickly uncovered a plethora of savory and sweet possibilities. In fact, the muffin pan is a kitchen workhorse if there ever were one. Don't let the name fool you; they're good for much more than rustling up a batch of muffins or cupcakes. After the assignment, I found myself breaking out the can-do pans more and more often for everything from individual quiches to pancakes. Here's why you should, too:

FAST AND FURIOUS. In many instances, cooking items in a muffin tin can significantly slash cooking time. Take mini meatloaves, for example. In a loaf pan, a meatloaf can take up to 1 hour to bake, but break up the portions into muffin cups and you can be feasting in half the time. Ditto for cakes and quick breads. This also helps cut down on energy usage, helping you save a few bucks and live a little greener.

BUILT-IN PORTION CONTROL. In a time when obesity is such a major concern, muffin tin meals are ideal for keeping portions in check. A recipe such as muffin-size frittatas may call for a cup of cheese (I mean, hey, isn't everything better with cheese?), but when the portion is just two individual frittatas, suddenly your fat and calorie intake is well within reason so your waistline won't bulge postprandial.

GREAT FOR KIDS. Preparing muffin-size items takes advantage of a child's preference for easy-to-grab, hand-to-mouth eating. Personal-size treats such as pizza or mac 'n' cheese are sure to be a hit at the dinner table and in the lunchroom. It's also easy to sneak in a bunch of vegetables that tykes may not be too enthusiastic about eating. And you can get them involved in mixing the ingredients and filling the muffin cups.

ADAPTABLE AND PACKABLE. Compact and portable, muffin tin meals are more transportable than their full-size counterparts, making them ideal for lunch boxes, road trips, potlucks, and picnics.

LOOKS TO KILL. If you're looking for an easy meal that will impress a group of family or friends, look no further! Adorable muffin tin meals and snacks are sure to be a conversation topic and make guests coo with delight.

FROZEN ASSETS. Stuck with extra chili, chicken broth, tomato paste, or pasta sauce? Instead of tossing these into a zip-top bag or plastic container where they'll form a giant food ice cube, try dividing them into muffin tin compartments. They'll freeze into individual portions that will defrost much quicker than a huge chunk of subzero food. Place items into the muffin cups, freeze until solid, unmold and then store in zip-top bags.

MY PERFECT DAY OF MUFFIN-SIZE EATING

If you asked me what my ideal day of noshing on muffin tin goodies would be, I would be in a state of edible bliss with this menu:

Breakfast: Peach Oatmeal Bake (page 23)

Morning Snack: Granola Rounds (page 37)

Lunch: Savory Smoked Salmon and Cheese Muffins (page 112)

Afternoon Snack: Seedy Rounds (page 38)

Dinner: Taco Cups (page 78)

Dessert: Extra-Moist Chocolate Cakes (page 122)

So you see, the muffin tin is undeniably a kitchenware overachiever. I hope you'll join me in the muffin tin revolution.

Tools of the Trade

Obviously, if you're going to give this book a good workout, you'll need an arsenal of muffin tins. Today, there are more options than ever.

Silicone

Love them or hate them, food-grade silicone muffin cups have a number of things going for them. Virtually nonstick, silicone is a smart choice for items that may adhere with passion to your muffin cups, such as egg-based quiches and frittatas. This cuts down on the need for using paper liners and the waste they create, as well as the need for greasing. I also appreciate that they're flexible, which makes unmolding goodies much less risky and arduous. You'll find this very helpful for recipes such as panna cottas (page 136) and the assortment of frozen treats, including the cappuccino cups (page 148). Being able to turn the cups inside out also makes washing them more manageable. However, you'll need to place silicone muffin trays on a baking sheet before sliding them into the oven to provide stability. Silicone is freezer-, microwave-, and dishwasher-safe, and the variety of cheerfully vibrant colors the trays come in can brighten up a kitchen.

However, there are a few caveats. Some manufacturers claim silicone does not stain. This has not been my experience with the colored trays. This is purely aesthetic and does not negatively affect performance. Silicone doesn't produce crispy pastry like metal or stoneware muffin tins do, so I'll often turn to the latter when making mini pies or other items with a crust. Depending on your preference, keep in mind that items such as cakes and muffins may not rise or brown to the same degree with silicone. Because you can't preheat them like you can with metal, silicone muffin cups are not ideal for recipes such as Yorkshire pudding (page 98) or popovers (page 37) where you want to add the batter to a hot pan.

By far, the best quality silicone muffin trays are the Flexipan ones from Demarle at Home, makers of the widely popular Silpat baking sheet liner. Made with a combination of woven glass and food-grade silicone, the shiny black trays produce better browning, rising, and more even cooking than other silicone muffin trays and are the most nonstick of the silicone bunch. They also can be rolled for easy storage. Bonus: They come with a lifetime warranty. For best results, Demarle recommends placing their trays on a perforated baking sheet, allowing more contact with the heat of the oven.

Metal

Standing the test of time, metal muffin trays remain the preferred choice for many home bakers. I recommend purchasing one made with heavy-gauge steel such as aluminized or stainless, which allow for even heating and produce perfectly browned baked items. When you pick up the pan, you want it to feel solid and have some weight to it. Also, look for a tin with large, wide handles, which make it easier to transport into and out of the oven. Nonstick coating makes unmolding and cleanup easier, but I understand that not everyone trusts that these materials are completely safe. Filling empty metal cups with water can help prevent scorching during baking.

Stoneware

I was skeptical at first, but I now adore my rustic Pampered Chef stoneware muffin tray. Made from clay, it produces reliable results since heat distribution is even and the nonporous surface doesn't retain odors. If not using paper liners, the more you use stoneware, the more "seasoned" and nonstick it becomes. Similar to cast-iron, it's best not to use soap for cleaning purposes. If you end up with sticky bits on the bottom, simply boil some water, pour it into the cups, and let it sit for several minutes to loosen.

Thick, dense stoneware holds its heat, meaning it can continue to cook whatever is in the muffin molds after removal from the oven. For this reason, I try to pull out items such as muffins and mini cakes a couple of minutes earlier than a recipe calls for to prevent overcooked and dried out baked goods. Like silicone, do not use stoneware under the broiler.

Cast-Iron

As they say, food just tastes better when cooked in heavy metal. Old-school cast-iron muffin trays produce crusty baked goods that brown nicely and evenly. Some cast-iron products such as those from Lodge come preseasoned for improved nonstick performance, but if you rescue one from Grandma's attic, you'll probably want to season it again for better results. Cast-iron holds its heat exceptionally well, so similar to baking in stoneware, err on the side of pulling items out of the oven a little early, as they'll continue to cook while sitting in the tray post-oven. As with all cast-iron cookware, a little loving care (don't wash with soap and dry immediately) goes a long way to ensure a lifetime of great performance. Since it's made out of iron, some of the mineral likely gets transferred to the food during baking. This is particularly beneficial for premenopausal women who often have poor iron levels due to menstrual blood loss and inadequate dietary intake.

Size Matters

Muffin tins generally come in three sizes: mini, medium, and jumbo.

Mini muffin trays that often have 12, 20, or 24 molds (holding about 2 tablespoons of batter each) per tray are great for making bite-size treats or a variety of crowd-friendly hors d'oeuvres.

Muffin trays with medium-size cups, sometimes called "standard" muffin trays, come with either 6 or 12 molds that hold about ½ cup each. This is the most versatile size for muffins, desserts, snack items, and savory side dishes.

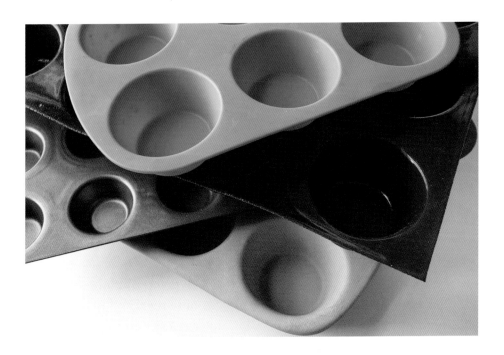

Jumbo, or Texas-size, muffin trays most often have 6 individual cup molds and each has about a 1-cup capacity. They are an excellent option for hearty muffin tin main dishes.

A Sticky Situation

It's completely deflating to put your heart into a recipe only to have huge chunks of it stick to the bottoms of the muffin cups. With the exception of silicone trays, which rarely need coating, greasing muffin cups with a moderate amount of oil or butter can often stymie serious sticking. This is particularly important for egg-based muffin tin creations such as frittatas, as eggs have the tendency to stick like cement. Be sure to get the oil or butter into all the crevices. After cooking, letting the items cool for several minutes in the muffin tray can go a long way in helping ensure intact extraction.

As long as you don't mind the fluted surface they leave, another option to reduce the worry of sticking is paper liners. Look for unbleached options, or better yet, try out the liners from PaperChef. Their parchment cups are very much nonstick and completely biodegradable. Or if you run out of liners, you can improvise with some parchment paper cut into squares, which can give items an elegant, Martha Stewart–worthy presentation. Greasing the muffin cups helps keep the parchment paper in place.

How to Use This Book

Accompanying many of the recipes on the following pages are these symbols:

- V Recipe is vegetarian, meaning it does not contain any meat or seafood. It may contain eggs or dairy.
- G Recipe is free of any gluten-containing products such as wheat flour. When purchasing items like oats or soy sauce, opt for those labeled "gluten-free."
- F Recipe can be frozen for later use.

Many recipes can be altered by substituting ingredients based on what's in your pantry and what your palate prefers. If you have special dietary needs, I'm confident you can work within the spirit of the recipe to make something similar that works for you. For example, if gluten tussles your tummy, you could use gluten-free bread crumbs or crushed puffed brown rice cereal when making individual shepherd's pies (page 90), or try textured vegetable protein when rustling up taco cups (page 78) to ensure they're vegetarian friendly.

Cooking times are approximate. Ovens can vary greatly with respect to the amount of heat they produce and retain. You may want to check for doneness about a minute or two before the cooking time indicated in the recipe. If your oven heats unevenly, try rotating the muffin tin halfway through the baking time.

Most often, I don't mention the need for greasing the muffin cups in the recipe instruction as this depends on the type of tray you use. For example, silicone trays rarely require it, but if using metal or stoneware, assume that it's always a good idea to apply a light coating of oil or butter. In reality, the extra calorie load this creates is negligible. I'm not a fan of oil sprays as they tend to leave a sticky residue and have an ingredient list with too many whatchamacallits. Better options for greasing are vegetables oils such as coconut or grapeseed and good old-fashioned butter. As the product cooks up, this little bit of fat on the bottom helps brown the undersides of baked goods, giving them a toasty mouthfeel. For intact extraction, always allow cooked items to cool in the muffin cups before attempting to un-mold.

As much as possible, I try to base recipes on whole foods, as these provide a bigger nutritional payoff than more processed ingredients. For example, I almost always try to swap out all-purpose flour for more nutrient-dense whole wheat pastry flour. More flavorful coconut palm sugar, called for in many recipes, is a definite step-up from heavily refined white sugar.

MORNING GLORIES: BREAKFAST & BRUNCH

As the old saying goes, "breakfast is the most important meal of the day." It's true! A raft of research shows that consuming a well-balanced breakfast can improve concentration and help one maintain a healthy body weight, the latter likely by revving up metabolism and helping you avoid vending machine temptation later in the day. Studies also suggest breakfast eaters have an overall diet that is richer in dietary fiber, vitamins, and minerals. But maybe you've fallen into a breakfast rut—serving up the same bowl of cereal or plate of fried eggs every morning has left you a little blasé about your daybreak meal. Well, these muffin tin breakfast ideas are a fun and tasty way to break out of it.

In a perfect world, we'd all sit down every morning to a leisurely, healthy breakfast. In the real world, however, most of us do our fair share of eating breakfast in the car, in front of the computer, or on the subway as mornings become a hectic blur of chores. Instead of picking up a calorie-bomb elephantine bagel or muffin on the go, opt for some of the recipes that follow such as baked oatmeal, bacon and egg cups, and orange popovers that are healthier alternatives when you're in a need for speed. Others, including polenta egg and sausage cups, and peach-stuffed French toast cups, are best enjoyed on a lazy weekend morning when you can afford the time to properly embrace their extra prep time and delightful flavors. Regardless, the heavy use of whole grains and smart protein choices within these recipes will give you sustained energy, not a short blast followed by a mid-morning crash.

BAKED EGGS IN PROSCIUTTO CUPS

Prosciutto is a thinly sliced cured ham originally from Italy and a wonderful alternative to bacon in this recipe. Unlike most muffin tin creations, these don't make good leftovers, so only prepare what you can eat at once. They can also anchor a dinner meal. Serve with a crusty bread for dipping into the runny yolks.   *Serves 3   G*

12 thin slices prosciutto

2 tablespoons grainy mustard or Dijon mustard

¼ cup finely chopped basil

⅓ cup grated Parmesan cheese (about 1 ounce)

6 large eggs

chopped fresh chives, for garnish

salt and pepper

Preheat the oven to 375°F. Grease 6 medium muffin cups with oil or butter and line each with 2 slices of prosciutto, enough to cover the bottom and sides completely. Spread mustard on the bottom of the prosciutto-lined cups, and top with basil and cheese. Press down lightly on the cheese to make room for the eggs.

Carefully crack an egg into each prosciutto cup. Season the tops of the eggs with salt and pepper. Place the muffin tray on a baking sheet to catch any egg overflow. Bake until the egg whites are set but the yolks are still slightly runny, about 17 minutes. Let cool for 5 minutes before unmolding. Garnish with fresh chives.

Top: BAKED EGGS IN PROSCIUTTO CUPS, *page 14*
Bottom: HUEVOS RANCHEROS WITH SALSA VERDE, *page 16*

HUEVOS RANCHEROS WITH SALSA VERDE

A classic Mexican breakfast, huevos rancheros are eggs served on hot corn tortillas and smothered in fiery salsa. Here, the tortilla cups hold all the contents in a neat little package that's vivified with the bright flavors of a tomatillo salsa.   *Serves 3   G, V*

6 (5-inch) corn tortillas

grapeseed or canola oil, as needed

1 cup canned pinto beans, drained and rinsed

½ teaspoon ground cumin

⅔ cup chopped fresh cilantro, divided

½ cup shredded pepper Jack cheese

6 large eggs, lightly beaten

Salsa:

8 to 10 fresh or canned husked tomatillos, finely diced

1 jalapeño or serrano chile pepper, seeded and finely diced

2 green onions, white and green parts, thinly sliced

2 garlic cloves, minced

grated zest and juice from ½ lime

sliced avocado, to serve (optional)

salt and pepper

Preheat the oven to 350°F. Heat the tortillas one at a time in a dry skillet over medium-high heat until soft and pliable, 15 to 20 seconds per side. Or, stack the tortillas and microwave on high power, uncovered, until warm and flexible, about 25 seconds. Brush both sides of the warm tortillas with oil. With the bottom of a glass, gently press the tortillas into 6 jumbo muffin cups. Don't worry if some of the tortilla folds inward.

In a medium bowl, mash together the pinto beans, cumin, and ⅓ cup of the cilantro with a potato masher or the back of a fork. Divide the bean mixture among the tortilla cups. Top each with an even amount of cheese and press down so there is room for the eggs. Pour the eggs evenly among the tortilla cups and season the tops with salt and pepper. Cook until the eggs have set, about 20 minutes. Let cool for several minutes before serving.

For the Salsa: To make the salsa, toss together the tomatillos, jalapeño or serrano pepper, green onions, garlic, lime zest and juice, and the remaining ⅓ cup cilantro. Season to taste with salt and pepper. Cook in a medium skillet over medium heat until the tomatillos have softened, about 5 minutes.

Serve the huevos rancheros cups topped with salsa verde, along with avocado and additional cilantro, if desired.

SPANISH OMELET

Traditional *tortilla Española*, or Spanish omelet, is a fairly bare-bones potato-based egg dish that somehow manages to rouse taste buds. However, this recipe expands on the classic ingredient list with the addition of lively tarragon and smoked paprika. Diced red bell pepper or zucchini would work well, too.   *Serves 6*   G, V

1 pound Yukon gold or red potatoes (about 3 medium)

2 tablespoons extra-virgin olive oil

1 yellow onion, finely chopped

6 large eggs, lightly beaten

2 tablespoons chopped fresh tarragon

½ teaspoon smoked paprika

¼ teaspoon salt

¼ teaspoon pepper

Peel the potatoes and cut into 1-inch cubes. Heat the olive oil in a large skillet over medium heat. Add the potatoes, and cook for 20 minutes, stirring occasionally. Add the onion and cook until potatoes are fork-tender, stirring occasionally, about 10 minutes more.

Preheat the oven to 350°F. Divide the potato-onion mixture among 12 medium muffin cups. In a medium bowl, mix together the eggs, tarragon, smoked paprika, salt, and pepper. Pour the egg mixture evenly over the potato mixture. Bake until the eggs are set, about 15 minutes. Let cool for several minutes before unmolding. Sprinkle with additional salt, if desired.

BACON AND EGGS

This play on a diner classic comes together easily and gets a nutrition boost from tomatoes, mushrooms, and peppery arugula. These can be stored in the fridge for a few days, making them a great option when you need a breakfast lickety-split. Make sure to remove the seeds from your tomatoes so the mixture doesn't become too watery. If possible, use nitrate-free, organic bacon. Serve with salsa or shredded aged cheddar cheese, if desired.   *Serves 6*   G

9 large eggs

½ pound bacon, cooked and diced

1 tomato, seeded and diced

2 green onions, white and green parts, sliced

1 cup diced cremini mushrooms

1 cup chopped arugula

1 tablespoon fresh thyme leaves

¼ teaspoon salt

¼ teaspoon pepper

Preheat the oven to 375°F. In a large bowl, lightly beat the eggs. Stir in the cooked bacon, tomato, green onions, mushrooms, arugula, thyme, salt, and pepper. Divide the mixture among 12 medium muffin cups and cook until set, about 20 minutes. Let cool for several minutes before unmolding.

EGG AND SAUSAGE POLENTA CUPS

Easy on the taste buds, polenta, eggs, and sausage add layers of loveliness to each bite. Even if using silicone muffin cups, make sure to use paper liners as the bottoms are quite moist, making intact removal without them a challenge. Also, it's best to avoid large eggs, which are too big for the cups and will cause overflow. Recipe can be doubled.   *Serves 3*   G

¾ cup low-fat milk

¾ cup water

½ cup corn grits (polenta)

⅔ cup shredded Asiago, Swiss, or fontina cheese (about 3 ounces)

2 tablespoons finely chopped fresh rosemary

½ teaspoon salt

2 teaspoons grapeseed or canola oil

3 ounces uncooked turkey sausage, casing removed, and chopped

6 small eggs

watercress or arugula, for garnish

Bring the milk and water to a slight simmer in a medium pot over medium heat.

Slowly whisk in the corn grits, and continue whisking until it begins to thicken and resemble creamy oatmeal, 3 to 4 minutes. Remove from the heat and stir in the cheese, rosemary, and salt. Let cool.

Heat the oil in a medium skillet over medium heat. Cook the sausage until lightly browned and no longer pink, about 3 minutes.

Preheat the oven to 400°F. Line 6 medium muffin cups with paper liners. Divide the polenta among the prepared muffin cups. Using your fingers, form a deep well in each one by pushing the polenta up the sides of the muffin cups. Crack an egg into each polenta cup and scatter the sausage on top. Place the muffin tin on a baking sheet to catch any egg overflow. Bake until the egg whites are firm but the yolks are still slightly runny, about 20 minutes. Let cool for several minutes before unmolding. Garnish with the watercress or arugula and additional shredded cheese, if desired.

COTTAGE CHEESE–PESTO MUFFINS

Who says pesto is just for sandwiches or pasta? These savory muffins are infused with protein-rich cottage cheese and nutritious almond flour to make them a wholesome breakfast.   *Serves 10   V, F*

1 cup whole wheat pastry flour or spelt flour

¾ cup almond flour

1 teaspoon baking powder

¼ teaspoon baking soda

1 tablespoon coconut palm sugar or other granulated sugar

2 large eggs

1 cup low-fat cottage cheese

⅓ cup melted coconut oil or other oil

3 tablespoons pesto

Preheat the oven to 350°F. In a large bowl, stir together the whole wheat pastry or spelt flour, almond flour, baking powder, baking soda, and sugar. In a medium bowl, whisk together the eggs, cottage cheese, oil, and pesto. Add the wet ingredients to the dry ingredients and stir gently. Divide the mixture among 10 medium muffin cups. Bake until an inserted toothpick comes out clean, about 20 minutes. Let cool for several minutes before unmolding.

BAKED OATMEAL

Why just eat your oatmeal from a bowl? Bake up a batch of these and you'll be set for a week's worth of nutritious breakfast meals. I prefer to use steel-cut oats as they're hearty and filling. Make these gluten-free by choosing oats labeled "gluten-free."   *Serves 6   V, F*

1 cup steel-cut oats
½ cup raisins
⅓ cup coarsely chopped walnuts
⅓ cup pumpkin seeds
⅓ cup ground flax seeds or chia seeds
1 teaspoon ground cinnamon, divided
½ teaspoon ground nutmeg

¼ teaspoon salt
2 large eggs
1½ cups low-fat milk
¼ cup natural smooth peanut butter
1 small unpeeled apple, finely chopped
pure maple syrup, to serve

In a medium bowl, cover the oats with water and soak overnight in the refrigerator.

Preheat the oven to 375°F. Drain the oats and add to a large bowl along with the raisins, walnuts, pumpkin seeds, flax seeds or chia seeds, ½ teaspoon of the cinnamon, and the nutmeg and salt. In a second large bowl, lightly beat the eggs, then beat in the milk and peanut butter. Add the dry ingredients to the wet ingredients and stir to combine. In a small bowl, toss together the apple and remaining ½ teaspoon cinnamon.

Divide the oat mixture among 12 medium muffin cups. Top each with an even amount of the apple-cinnamon mixture. Bake until an inserted toothpick comes out clean, about 20 minutes. Serve with a generous drizzle of maple syrup.

PEACH OATMEAL BAKE

When life gives you peaches, rustle up a batch of these gems. These look (and taste!) like they're much more of a high-flying kitchen feat than they are. Make these gluten-free by using "gluten-free" oats.   *Serves 6*   *V*

⅔ cup unsalted raw cashews

2 cups quick-cook rolled oats (not instant)

1 cup low-fat milk or unflavored nondairy milk

2 large eggs

2 tablespoons honey

1 teaspoon ground cinnamon

¼ teaspoon ground cloves

1 teaspoon almond extract

1 teaspoon vanilla extract

⅓ cup chopped almonds

⅓ cup dried currants

1 large peach, pitted and sliced

1 tablespoon coconut palm sugar or brown sugar, or as needed

To make cashew cream, place the cashews in a bowl, cover with water, and soak for at least 2 hours. Drain the cashews and place in a blender with just enough fresh water to barely cover the nuts. Blend until smooth.

Preheat the oven to 350°F. In a large bowl, stir together the cashew cream, oats, milk, eggs, honey, cinnamon, cloves, almond extract, and vanilla extract. Fold in the almonds and currants.

Divide the mixture among 6 jumbo muffin cups and top each with 2 peach slices. Sprinkle the tops with sugar and bake until the oatmeal is set, about 30 minutes. Let cool for several minutes before unmolding.

GERMAN PEAR PANCAKES

Tender baked German pancakes fall somewhere between a crepe and an American flapjack, and adapt very well to the muffin tin. Traditionally, they're made with apples, but this recipe is a great way to use seasonal pears.   *Serves 4*   *V*

2 medium ripe pears

¼ cup plus 1 tablespoon coconut palm sugar or other granulated sugar, divided

½ teaspoon ground cinnamon

1 tablespoon lemon juice

½ cup whole wheat pastry flour

⅓ cup almond flour

3 large eggs

2 tablespoons melted unsalted butter, cooled

¾ cup low-fat milk

¼ teaspoon ground cloves

¼ teaspoon salt

pure maple syrup, to serve

Preheat the oven to 400°F. Slice the pears into wedges, then cut each wedge into 4 pieces. In a medium bowl, toss the pears with 1 tablespoon of the sugar and the cinnamon and lemon juice.

In a blender or food processor, puree the remaining ¼ cup sugar and the whole wheat pastry flour, almond flour, eggs, melted butter, milk, cloves, and salt until well combined and smooth. Divide the pears among 12 medium muffin cups and pour the batter over the top. Bake until puffed, about 15 minutes. Let cool for several minutes before unmolding. Serve with maple syrup.

Top: GERMAN PEAR PANCAKES, *page 24*
Bottom: PEACH-STUFFED FRENCH TOAST BOWLS, *page 26*

PEACH-STUFFED FRENCH TOAST BOWLS WITH VANILLA-SCENTED YOGURT

Local peaches, egg-soaked bread, and vanilla-spiked creamy Greek yogurt team up in this riff on iconic French toast. They may look difficult to make, but they're really not. It's best to use jumbo muffin cups as they are easier to fit the bread into. If desired, stir some maple syrup into the yogurt.   *Serves 3   V*

6 slices whole-grain bread

4 large eggs

2 tablespoons low-fat milk

2 tablespoons coconut palm sugar or other granulated sugar, divided

1 teaspoon ground cinnamon, divided

¼ teaspoon ground nutmeg

3 medium peaches, diced

1 tablespoon lemon juice

½ cup low-fat Greek yogurt

1 teaspoon vanilla extract

Preheat the oven to 375°F. Gently flatten the bread slices with a rolling pin to about ¼ inch thick. In a flat-bottomed bowl, lightly beat the eggs, milk, 1 tablespoon of the sugar, ½ teaspoon of the cinnamon, and the nutmeg. One at a time, soak the bread slices in the egg mixture for 10 seconds per side, letting the excess drip off. Gently press into 6 jumbo muffin cups, forming a cup shape. Bake until the bread is crisp, about 14 minutes.

Meanwhile, in a large bowl, toss together the peaches, lemon juice, remaining 1 tablespoon sugar, and remaining ½ teaspoon cinnamon. Heat the peach mixture in a large nonstick skillet over medium heat until the peaches have softened, about 5 minutes. Stir together the yogurt and vanilla extract in a small bowl. Divide the peach mixture among the French toast cups and top with vanilla yogurt.

MICROWAVE QUINOA CAKES WITH MAPLE-ALMOND BUTTER

Armed with silicone muffin cups, you can whip up quick, and surprisingly good, whole-grain breakfast cakes (slash) muffins in the now-ubiquitous microwave. Don't try these with metal tins! You can cook the quinoa the night before or use leftover cooked quinoa from another recipe. Take these cakes up a notch by bejeweling them with the creamy maple-almond topping.   *Serves 3   G, V, F*

1 medium banana

½ cup cooked white quinoa

2 large eggs

2 tablespoons raisins

2 tablespoons coconut palm sugar or other granulated sugar

½ teaspoon ground cinnamon

¼ teaspoon ground nutmeg

½ teaspoon baking powder

¼ teaspoon almond extract

2 tablespoons unsalted smooth almond butter

2 tablespoons pure maple syrup

In a large bowl, mash the banana. Stir in the quinoa, eggs, raisins, sugar, cinnamon, nutmeg, baking powder, and almond extract. Divide the batter among 6 medium silicone muffin cups, filling each about two-thirds full. Microwave on high power until set, about 2½ minutes, rotating the cups once halfway through cooking if needed. In a small bowl, stir together the almond butter and maple syrup. Serve the cakes topped with almond-maple butter.

FRENCH TOASTIES WITH BLUEBERRY COMPOTE

French toast is the epitome of casual breakfast fare. This whimsical twist on a breakfast classic hits all the right flavor notes: sweet, warming, and toasty. *Serves 4* *V, F*

French Toast:
6 slices whole-grain bread

3 large eggs

⅓ cup plus 2 tablespoons low-fat milk

1 tablespoon coconut palm sugar or other granulated sugar

1 teaspoon vanilla extract

¼ teaspoon ground cardamom

¼ teaspoon salt

Blueberry Compote:
1 cup fresh or frozen blueberries

⅓ cup pure maple syrup

½ teaspoon ground cinnamon

1 teaspoon grated orange zest

1 teaspoon cornstarch

For the French Toast: Cut the bread into 1-inch cubes. In a large bowl, lightly beat the eggs, then beat in the milk, sugar, vanilla extract, cardamom, and salt. Stir in the bread cubes until they are all moist. Let sit for 5 minutes.

Preheat the oven to 350°F. Divide the bread cubes among 12 medium muffin cups and pour any leftover egg mixture on top. Bake until they start turning golden on top and the egg has set, about 22 minutes.

For the Blueberry Compote: While the French toast bakes, in a small saucepan over medium-high heat, stir together the blueberries, maple syrup, cinnamon, and orange zest. Bring to a boil, reduce the heat to medium-low, and simmer for 5 minutes. Stir in the cornstarch and simmer until slightly thickened, about 1 minute more. Serve the French toasties topped with the blueberry compote.

Top: FRENCH TOASTIES WITH BLUEBERRY COMPOTE, *page 28*
Bottom: PARMESAN HASH BROWNS, *page 30*

PARMESAN HASH BROWNS

With their crispy exterior and moist tender interior, iconic hash browns are hard to resist. Especially this gussied up version—the mustard is a must! Some supermarkets sell bagged shredded potatoes in the refrigerator section, which can be a time saver. *Serves 4* V, G

4 cups peeled and shredded white potatoes (about 2 large)

½ cup grated Parmesan cheese (about 2 ounces)

2 tablespoons fresh thyme or 1 teaspoon dried thyme

2 tablespoons extra-virgin olive oil

2 teaspoons grainy mustard

1 teaspoon garlic powder

1 shallot, finely chopped

low-fat sour cream, to serve (optional)

salt and pepper

Preheat the oven to 375°F. In batches, roll the shredded potato in a clean kitchen towel or between a few sheets of paper towel and press out as much water as possible. In a large bowl, toss together the potatoes, Parmesan cheese, thyme, olive oil, mustard, garlic powder, and shallot. Season to taste with salt and pepper.

Divide the mixture among 12 medium muffin cups and lightly press on each to pack down. Bake until the edges begin to brown, about 45 minutes.

Let rest for several minutes, and gently lift the hash brown cups out of the muffin cups. Serve with a dollop of sour cream, if desired.

TURKEY-PARMESAN MUFFINS

This is definitely one of my favorite savory muffin recipes. The turkey and Parmesan team up to create a powerful flavor punch. Because recipes are only as good as their ingredients, make sure to use a high-quality Parmesan. These contain meat, so make sure to store them in the fridge.   *Serves 12*
V, F

1 tablespoon grapeseed or canola oil

1 pound turkey sausage

1½ cups whole wheat pastry flour or spelt flour

3 tablespoons finely chopped fresh rosemary

1 tablespoon coconut palm sugar or other granulated sugar

1 teaspoon baking powder

¼ teaspoon baking soda

¼ teaspoon salt

2 large eggs

1 cup grated Parmesan cheese (about 4 ounces)

3 garlic cloves, grated or very finely minced

1 cup plain low-fat or whole milk yogurt

¼ cup low-fat milk

¼ cup melted coconut oil or other oil

Heat the oil in a large skillet over medium heat. Remove the sausage from its casing, crumble into the skillet, and cook until brown. Make sure the sausage is in small pieces. Let cool.

In a large bowl, stir together the flour, rosemary, sugar, baking powder, baking soda, and salt. In a medium bowl, lightly beat the eggs. Stir in the Parmesan cheese, garlic, yogurt, milk, and oil. Add the wet ingredients to the dry ingredients and stir gently to combine. Fold in the cooked sausage. Divide the mixture among 12 medium muffin cups and bake until an inserted toothpick comes out clean, about 20 minutes. Let cool for several minutes before unmolding.

HOT CROSS CRANBERRY BUNS

Rich in gustatory romance and traditionally served on Good Friday, hot cross buns are basically sweet yeast dough mixed with warming spices and raisins (I prefer cranberries!), and then finished off with a cross. So delightful, there's no reason to relegate these to only Easter weekend.   *Serves 8   V, F*

¾ cup plus 2 tablespoons low-fat milk

½ cup plus 1 teaspoon coconut palm sugar or other granulated sugar, divided

1½ cups whole wheat pastry flour, divided

1 packet (2¼ teaspoons) active dry yeast

1½ cups all-purpose flour or bread flour

1 teaspoon salt

½ teaspoon ground nutmeg

½ teaspoon ground cinnamon

¼ teaspoon ground allspice

1 cup dried cranberries

¼ cup (½ stick) unsalted butter, melted and cooled

2 large whole eggs, at room temperature, lightly beaten

2 large egg whites, divided

a splash of milk

2 cups confectioners' sugar, or as needed

In a small saucepan, scald the milk by heating it over medium heat until bubbles form around the edges. In a large bowl, stir together the hot milk with 1 teaspoon of the coconut palm or other granulated sugar, ¾ cup of the whole wheat pastry flour, and the yeast. Set aside until frothy, about 15 minutes.

In a second large bowl, sift together the remaining ¾ cup whole wheat pastry flour and the all-purpose or bread flour, salt, nutmeg, cinnamon, and allspice. Stir in the remaining ½ cup coconut palm or other granulated sugar and the cranberries. Add the yeast mixture, butter, and whole eggs, and stir to combine. Turn the dough onto a well-floured work surface and knead until the dough is smooth and stretchy but a little bit sticky, about 10 minutes. Place the dough in a large bowl and cover with a clean kitchen towel. Place in a warm, draft-free place until the dough doubles in size, about 1 hour.

Punch the dough down in the middle with your fist. Turn the dough onto a floured surface and knead for 3 minutes more. Divide the dough into 16 even pieces, shape each portion into a ball, and drop into 16 medium muffin cups. Cover with a kitchen towel and set aside in a warm, draft-free place for 30 minutes.

Preheat the oven to 350°F. To make the glaze, mix 1 egg white with the milk and brush onto each bun. Bake until the tops of the buns have turned golden brown, about 20 minutes. Let cool for several minutes before unmolding.

To make the icing cross, place the remaining 1 egg white in a medium bowl and add ½ cup of the confectioners' sugar. Beat with an electric mixer on medium speed until smooth. Keep adding confectioners' sugar ¼ cup at a time until you achieve a very thick, smooth, white icing. Pipe the "cross" on each bun using a piping bag or a small zip-top bag with a corner cut off.

ORANGE POPOVERS WITH RASPBERRY-CHIA JAM

A popover is a light, hollow roll made from an egg flour batter and traditionally served at breakfast or brunch in Britain. If you don't have a popover tin, metal muffin tins will certainly do the job adequately.
Serves 6   V, F

Raspberry Chia Jam:
2 tablespoons chia seeds
1½ cups water
1½ cups raspberries
1½ tablespoons coconut palm sugar or other granulated sugar

Popovers:
3 large eggs
1½ cups low-fat milk

¾ cup whole wheat pastry flour
¾ cup all-purpose flour
2 teaspoons coconut palm sugar or other granulated sugar
1 teaspoon ground cinnamon
2 teaspoons grated orange zest
½ teaspoon salt
2 tablespoons unsalted butter, melted

For the Raspberry Chia Jam: In a small bowl, whisk together the chia seeds and water. Let sit for at least 30 minutes to form a gel, stirring with a whisk occasionally to prevent clumping. Place the chia seed gel in a blender or food processor along with the raspberries and sugar. Blend or process until just combined. Refrigerate overnight before serving.

For the Popovers: Grease 12 medium muffin cups with butter. Turn the oven to 450°F and place the muffin tin in the oven to preheat while you make the batter.

Place all of the popover ingredients in a blender in the order given. Puree until mixed, about 30 seconds. When the oven is preheated, remove the hot muffin tin and fill the cups about two-thirds full with batter. Bake for 20 minutes. Reduce the temperature to 350°F and bake for another 10 minutes. Don't open the oven door any time during baking! Allow the popovers to cool in the tin for several minutes before unmolding. Serve warm with the raspberry chia jam.

Top: ORANGE POPOVERS WITH RASPBERRY-CHIA JAM, *page 34*
Bottom: APRICOT JAM—STUFFED BREAD CUPS, *page 36*

APRICOT JAM—STUFFED BREAD CUPS

This riff on toast and jam is sure to impress your table mates. Farm-fresh apricots, sugar, lemon, and cardamom mingle to create a flavor nirvana. The jam can be made ahead of time and kept in the fridge for up to two weeks. You can also use store-bought apricot jam, if desired, and use gluten-free bread if needed. *Serves 6*   *V*

1 pound fresh apricots (about 12), sliced in half and pitted

¼ cup plus 2 tablespoons coconut palm sugar or other granulated sugar

½ teaspoon grated lemon zest

1 tablespoon lemon juice

1 teaspoon vanilla extract

½ teaspoon almond extract

¼ teaspoon ground cardamom

12 slices raisin bread

grapeseed or canola oil, as needed

½ cup chopped almonds

In a medium saucepan over medium heat, stir together the apricots, sugar, lemon zest, lemon juice, vanilla extract, almond extract, and cardamom until the sugar dissolves, about 2 minutes. Cover and refrigerate for several hours to allow the fruit to macerate and the flavors to meld.

Bring the apricot mixture to a boil over medium-high heat, reduce the heat to low, and simmer, covered, until the fruit has broken down and the mixture resembles chunky jam, about 75 minutes. Stir the mixture about every 15 minutes.

Preheat the oven to 350°F. Flatten the bread slices with a rolling pin to about ¼ inch thick. Slice the bread into 12 rounds using a cookie cutter or the top of a glass that is about the same size as a medium muffin cup. Brush both sides of each round with oil, and carefully press into 12 medium muffin cups. Bake until crispy and golden, about 8 minutes.

Meanwhile, toast the almonds in a dry skillet over medium heat until darkened, about 4 minutes, stirring often. To serve, fill the bread cups with apricot jam and top with toasted almonds.

GRANOLA ROUNDS

Although granola bars aren't usually round, what the heck? Packed with wholesome ingredients, these are perfect energy for the trail or a mid-morning boost.   *Serves 12   V, F*

1½ cups quick-cook rolled oats (not instant)

½ cup almond flour

½ cup ground flax seeds or ground chia seeds

½ cup coarsely chopped walnuts

¼ cup sunflower seeds

½ cup dried blueberries

½ cup dried cranberries

⅓ cup unsweetened dried coconut

½ teaspoon ground cinnamon

½ teaspoon salt

¼ teaspoon ground allspice

1 large egg

⅔ cup honey

¼ cup melted coconut oil or other oil

1 teaspoon vanilla extract

½ teaspoon almond extract (optional)

Preheat the oven to 350°F. In a large bowl, stir together the oats, almond flour, flax seeds or chia seeds, walnuts, sunflower seeds, blueberries, cranberries, coconut, cinnamon, salt, and allspice. In a separate bowl, lightly beat the egg and stir in the honey, oil, vanilla extract, and almond extract, if using. Add the wet ingredients to the dry ingredients and stir until everything is moist. Divide the mixture among 12 medium muffin cups and pack down tightly with the back of a spoon to help keep them together after baking. Bake until the edges begin to brown, about 20 minutes. Let cool for several minutes before unmolding.

SEEDY ROUNDS

Not just for the birds, these seedy little packages of energy and nutrients are fit for humans and provide good motivation to raid the bulk bins. If you're as concerned with genetically modified foods as I am, choose organic corn syrup to assure that no GM corn was used. If you're not using a silicone muffin tray, it's best to use paper liners.   *Serves 9   V, G, F*

⅓ cup quinoa

⅓ cup sunflower seeds

¼ cup black sesame seeds

¼ cup hemp seeds

¼ cup pumpkin seeds

2 tablespoons chia seeds

⅓ cup chopped pecans

¼ teaspoon salt

¼ cup light corn syrup

¼ cup pure maple syrup, preferably a darker grade

Preheat the oven to 350°F. In a dry skillet, toast the quinoa over medium heat until it gives off a toasted aroma and begins to pop, about 3 minutes. Stir often to prevent burning. In a large bowl, stir together the toasted quinoa, sunflower seeds, sesame seeds, hemp seeds, pumpkin seeds, chia seeds, pecans, and salt. In a medium saucepan, heat the corn syrup and maple syrup over medium heat until hot, 2 to 3 minutes. Stir in the seed mixture and mix until everything is moist. Divide the mixture among 18 mini muffin cups and press down with damp fingers to tightly compact the contents. Bake for 15 minutes and let cool for several minutes before unmolding. They will harden while they cool, helping them to stick together.

FRUITY ENERGY BITES

These bites are packed with natural sugars, and I'll grab a couple before my bicycle rides for an energy boost. They also work perfectly well as a snack if I'm desk-bound.   *Serves 12   V, G, F*

1½ cup pitted dried dates, chopped
1 cup dried Mission figs, chopped
1 cup dried apricots, chopped
½ cup shelled unsalted pistachios
⅓ cup hemp seeds
¼ cup brown rice syrup

2 tablespoons unsweetened cocoa powder
½ teaspoon salt
2 teaspoons grated orange zest
1 teaspoon vanilla extract or coffee extract

In a food processor, process the dates, figs, apricots, pistachios, and hemp seeds until finely chopped. Add the brown rice syrup, cocoa, salt, orange zest, and vanilla or coffee extract, and process until the mixture clumps together. Pack the mixture into 24 mini muffin cups and freeze until firm, about 30 minutes. Unmold and store in the refrigerator in an airtight container.

ALMOND PROTEIN BITES

Pop a couple of these and you'll get plenty of healthy fats and protein to quell hunger pangs. Hemp protein provides an earthy element that I enjoy, and the creamy deliciousness of almond butter is hard to beat. If using plain protein powder, you can mix in 1 teaspoon vanilla extract.

Serves 8   V, G, F

¾ cup unsalted smooth almond butter

¼ cup honey, agave syrup, or brown rice syrup, or as needed

¾ cup granola

¾ cup vanilla hemp protein powder or other protein powder

⅓ cup raisins

⅓ cup chopped almonds

2 tablespoons cocoa nibs (optional)

2 tablespoons unsweetened shredded coconut (optional)

½ teaspoon ground cinnamon

Place all the ingredients in a large bowl and stir with a rubber spatula until the protein powder and granola are incorporated. Taste and adjust the sweetness with more honey, agave syrup, or brown rice syrup as needed. Pack the mixture into 16 mini muffin cups and place in the freezer for 30 minutes to harden slightly. Unmold and store in the refrigerator in an airtight container.

SPLENDID STARTERS: APPETIZERS

Want to impress guests and start a festive gathering with something other than the same old cheese plate? Here are a handful of fun mini muffin tin appetizers that offer the perfect trifecta: great flavor, nutritional perks, and just the right note of elegance. They are the perfect little bites for parties, potlucks, joyful family gatherings, or the big game and are sure to fly off of your appetizer tray. Or do as I did when plugging away at these recipes—combine a few and serve up an appetizer-filled dinner. Kids will eat it up! If entertaining a smaller crowd, each of these recipes can be halved.

CURRIED SHRIMP CUPS

Each bite of these is like a festival of flavors in your mouth and a great way to kick off an evening of entertaining. If you're jonesing to make these ahead of time, you can refrigerate the shrimp mixture for up to a day. Look for small, square wonton wrappers at most grocery stores and Asian markets.   *Serves 6 to 12*

24 wonton wrappers

2 teaspoons grapeseed or canola oil

½ cup plain low-fat yogurt

¼ cup chopped cilantro

juice of ½ lime

1½ teaspoons grated fresh ginger

1 teaspoon curry powder

½ teaspoon ground cumin

⅛ teaspoon cayenne pepper or chili powder

2 green onions, white and green parts, thinly sliced

1 pound cooked shrimp, coarsely chopped

salt and black pepper

Preheat the oven to 375°F. Using a pastry brush, lightly coat both sides of the wonton wrappers with the oil. Press each wrapper into 24 mini muffin cups, making sure the bottoms are as flat as possible. Lightly sprinkle with salt and bake until golden and crisp, about 10 minutes. Carefully remove the wrappers from the muffin cups and cool completely on a wire rack.

In a large bowl, stir together the yogurt, cilantro, lime juice, ginger, curry powder, cumin, cayenne pepper or chili powder, green onions, and salt and black pepper to taste. Stir in the shrimp and mix well. Divide the shrimp mixture among the wonton cups and serve.

Top: CURRIED SHRIMP CUPS, *page 42*

Bottom: GOAT CHEESE—MUSHROOM PHYLLO BITES, *page 44*

GOAT CHEESE—MUSHROOM PHYLLO BITES

This elegant appetizer (or side dish) gets a salty kick from the capers and a creamy finish from the goat cheese.   *Serves 6 to 12   V*

1 tablespoon unsalted butter

8 ounces chopped assorted mushrooms such as oyster, shiitake, and cremini (about 3 cups)

1 leek, thinly sliced

1 tablespoon fresh thyme

1 tablespoon capers, drained

4 sheets phyllo pastry, thawed

grapeseed or canola oil or melted butter, as needed

4 ounces soft goat cheese

salt and pepper

Heat the butter in a medium skillet over medium heat. Add the mushrooms, leek, and salt and pepper to taste. Cook just until the mushrooms are softened, about 4 minutes. Stir in the thyme and capers. Set aside.

Preheat the oven to 350°F. Very carefully place one sheet of phyllo pastry on a work surface and cover the remaining sheets with a damp kitchen towel to keep them from drying out. Brush oil or melted butter over the surface of the phyllo sheet and cover with another sheet of phyllo. Brush with oil or butter and repeat with another 2 phyllo sheets so you have 4 layers. With the tip of a sharp knife or pizza cutter, carefully cut the layered sheets into 6 equal segments from top to bottom and then at the midway point from left to right to form 12 squares. Cut each square in half to form 24 rectangles. Stuff the phyllo into 24 mini muffin cups and place a dollop of goat cheese in each. Divide the mushroom mixture evenly among the muffin cups. Bake until the phyllo is crisp and browned on the edges, about 8 minutes. Let cool for several minutes before unmolding.

PROSCIUTTO CHEESE PUFFS

Salty and cheesy, with a fiery bite. Beautiful! If you're serving any gluten-sensitive individuals, use gluten-free flour such as brown rice.   *Serves 6 to 12*

2 tablespoons unsalted butter

4 tablespoons whole wheat flour

¾ cup low-fat milk

4 large eggs, separated

3 ounces finely chopped prosciutto

2 serrano or jalapeño peppers, seeded and finely chopped

¾ cup shredded sharp cheddar cheese (about 3 ounces)

1 tablespoon grainy or Dijon mustard

½ teaspoon salt

¼ teaspoon pepper

Grease 12 mini muffin cups with butter and sprinkle flour into each. Tap out any excess flour. In a medium saucepan, melt the butter over medium-high heat. Add the flour and cook, whisking constantly, until the mixture is lightly golden, about 2 minutes. (You're fundamentally making a roux.) Whisk in the milk, remove the pan from the heat, and stir in the egg yolks, prosciutto, jalapeño or serrano peppers, cheddar cheese, mustard, salt, and pepper. The mixture will be thick. Let cool to about room temperature.

Preheat the oven to 400°F. In a medium bowl with a whisk or an electric mixer on medium speed, beat the egg whites until soft peaks form. Stir one-quarter of the egg whites into the prosciutto mixture, then gently fold in the remaining egg whites. Divide the mixture among the prepared muffin cups and bake until puffed and set, about 10 minutes. Let cool for 5 minutes before unmolding. They will fall upon cooling.

TWO-CHEESE SMOKY CHICKEN CUPS

The smoky heat from the chipotle chiles really turns things up a notch. Sour cream provides some cooling relief for guests who are heat sensitive. Look for canned chipotle chile peppers in adobo sauce in the Latin section of your grocer. It's such a versatile flavor booster and a little goes a long way, so it's one of those items worth ordering online if you can't find it locally.   *Serves 6 to 12*

1 cup cooked chicken, shredded or finely diced

3 green onions, white and green parts, thinly sliced

½ cup finely chopped tomatoes, seeded and diced

½ cup finely chopped red bell pepper

1 tablespoon apple cider vinegar

2 teaspoons minced canned chipotle chile in adobo sauce

24 wonton wrappers

grapeseed or canola oil, as needed

⅔ cup shredded mozzarella cheese (about 3 ounces)

⅔ cup shredded cheddar cheese (about 3 ounces)

½ cup reduced-fat sour cream

1 teaspoon grated lime zest

juice of ½ lime

salt and pepper

Preheat the oven to 375°F. In a large bowl, toss together the chicken, green onions, tomatoes, bell pepper, apple cider vinegar, chipotle chile, and salt and pepper to taste. With a pastry brush, lightly coat both sides of the wonton wrappers with oil. Press the wrappers into 24 mini muffin cups, making sure the bottoms are as flat as possible. Place a small amount of mozzarella cheese in each cup. Top with the chicken mixture and then the cheddar cheese. Bake until the wonton wrappers are golden and crisp, about 10 minutes. Let cool for several minutes before unmolding.

In a small bowl, stir the together sour cream, lime zest, and lime juice. Serve alongside the chicken cups.

Top: TWO-CHEESE SMOKY CHICKEN CUPS, *page 46*
Bottom: SPINACH DIP BOWLS, *page 48*

SPINACH DIP BOWLS

Chips and dip are a big part of party fare. For the bowls, you can also use naan bread or even store-bought pizza crust.   *Serves 6 to 12   V*

2 loaves flatbread, preferably whole-grain

grapeseed or canola oil, as needed

6 ounces spinach (about 1 large bunch)

½ cup canned or jarred artichoke hearts

½ cup reduced-fat ricotta cheese

¼ cup reduced-fat sour cream

2 garlic cloves, grated or finely minced

½ teaspoon grated lemon zest

¼ teaspoon ground nutmeg

dash or two of cayenne pepper, or a few squirts of hot sauce

salt and black pepper

Preheat the oven to 375°F. Cut 24 (2-inch) rounds from the flatbread using a cookie cutter, the top of a glass, a ¼-cup metal measure, or similar object that is about the same size as the top of a mini muffin cup. Brush both sides of each round with oil and carefully press into 24 mini muffin cups, making sure the bottoms are flat. Bake until crispy, about 8 minutes.

Meanwhile, blanch the spinach by bringing a large pot of water to a boil and filling a large bowl with ice water. Add the spinach to the pot and boil until bright green in color, about 30 seconds. Drain and place in the ice water for about 2 minutes. Drain and squeeze out as much liquid as possible between sheets of paper towel or a clean kitchen towel. Chop the spinach finely. Place the artichoke hearts between sheets of paper towel and press to remove excess liquid. Chop the artichoke hearts finely and place in a large bowl along with the spinach, ricotta cheese, sour cream, garlic, lemon zest, nutmeg, cayenne pepper or hot sauce, and salt and black pepper to taste. Stir to combine well.

Remove the muffin tin from oven and stuff each bread cup with the spinach mixture. Cover with aluminum foil, return to the oven and bake for 10 minutes. Let cool for 5 minutes before unmolding, and serve.

BASIL PESTO

You can use store-bought pesto for the caprese cups on page 50, but making your own will almost always produce more flavorful results. And it's so simple! Use extras in pasta or sandwiches, mixed with cooked potatoes, or freeze in your mini muffin cups.   *Makes about ¾ cup*   F

1 cup tightly packed fresh basil leaves

2 garlic cloves, chopped

¼ cup coarsely chopped walnuts

⅓ cup grated Parmigiano-Reggiano or Parmesan cheese (about 1½ ounces)

juice of ½ lemon

¼ teaspoon salt

¼ cup extra-virgin olive oil

Place the basil, garlic, and walnuts in the bowl of a food processor and pulse a few times until coarsely minced. Add the Parmigiano-Reggiano or Parmesan cheese, lemon juice, and salt, and process until combined. Scrape the sides of the bowl. With the processor running, add the olive oil through the feed tube until fully combined.

CAPRESE CUPS

Caprese is an Italian sandwich or salad made predominantly with tomatoes, mozzarella, and basil. This spin is fit for a crowd and a lot less messy than that other Italian favorite, bruschetta. If possible, use buffalo mozzarella, which is most often sold in containers with water. The prepared cups can be assembled a day in advance and kept in the refrigerator. You can also make these a side dish by cutting bigger tortilla rounds and using medium-size muffin cups.   *Serves 6 to 12*   V

8 (6-inch) whole wheat tortillas

grapeseed or canola oil, as needed

3 ounces fresh mozzarella, finely chopped

⅓ cup Basil Pesto (see page 49)

2 plum (Roma) tomatoes, finely diced

1 tablespoon extra-virgin olive oil

salt

Preheat the oven to 375°F. Slice the tortillas into rounds about 2½ inches wide using a cookie cutter, the top of a glass, or the top of a metal ⅓-cup measure. You should get 3 rounds per tortilla, and you want them to be slightly larger than the tops of mini muffin cup molds. Brush each tortilla round with oil and place them over the tops of 24 mini muffin cups. Top each round with an equal amount of mozzarella, pesto (about ¼ teaspoon), and tomatoes. Press each round into the muffin cups molds to form cups. The contents help keep the tortilla rounds in place. Sprinkle each with a pinch of salt. Bake until the tortilla cups are crispy and golden, about 10 minutes. Place the caprese cups on a serving platter and drizzle with olive oil.

Top: CAPRESE CUPS, *page 50*

Bottom: SMOKED MACKEREL MOUSSE CUPS, *page 52*

SMOKED MACKEREL MOUSSE CUPS

Inexpensive omega-3-plush smoked mackerel is available at most well-stocked fishmongers. Horseradish gives each bite some zing, while a smooth and creamy consistency will assure your guests never need to know that you used low-fat versions of ricotta and sour cream. *Serves 6 to 12*

1 pound smoked mackerel fillets

⅔ cup reduced-fat ricotta cheese

⅔ cup reduced-fat sour cream

juice of ½ lemon

1 shallot, chopped

1 tablespoon horseradish

2 tablespoons chopped chives, plus more for garnish

¼ teaspoon pepper

4 phyllo sheets, thawed

grapeseed or canola oil or melted butter, as needed

Lift the mackerel flesh away from skin and place in a food processor along with the ricotta cheese, sour cream, lemon, shallot, horseradish, chives, and pepper. Process until smooth, stopping halfway if needed to scrape the mixture down the sides of the bowl. Refrigerate until cold.

Preheat the oven to 350°F. Very carefully place one sheet of phyllo pastry on a work surface and cover the remaining sheets with a damp kitchen towel to keep them moist. Brush the oil or melted butter over the surface of the sheet and cover with another sheet of phyllo. Brush with more oil or butter and repeat with another 2 phyllo sheets so you have 4 layers. With the tip of a sharp knife or a pizza cutter, carefully cut the layered sheets into 3 segments from top to bottom and then slice from left to right at the midway point to make 6 total squares. Slice each square in half to make a total of 12 phyllo rectangles. Tuck the phyllo into 12 medium muffin cups, making sure the bottoms are flat. Bake until crispy and golden, 10 to 12 minutes, watching carefully so they don't burn.

Spoon the mackerel mousse into the phyllo cups and garnish with additional chives.

CRUSTLESS SMOKED SALMON QUICHES

These fuss-free, delicious quiches will go missing from a party tray in no time. They can be cooked in advance and kept in the refrigerator for a couple of days to be reheated when required. Resist the urge to add much, if any, salt as the smoked salmon and capers already do the job for you.   *Serves 6 to 12   G*

4 large eggs

½ cup low-fat sour cream

1 tablespoon capers, drained

2 tablespoons fresh dill, plus more for garnish

2 teaspoons grainy or Dijon mustard

juice of ½ lemon

2 garlic cloves, minced

2 green onions, white and green parts, thinly sliced

¼ teaspoon pepper

3 ounces smoked salmon, finely chopped

Preheat the oven to 350°F. Grease 24 mini muffin cups with butter. In a large bowl, gently beat the eggs. Stir in the sour cream, capers, dill, mustard, lemon juice, garlic, green onions, and pepper. Mix in the smoked salmon. Divide the mixture evenly among the prepared muffin cups and bake until the quiches are set, about 15 minutes. Let cool for 5 minutes before unmolding. Serve garnished with additional dill, if desired.

FALAFELS WITH ASPARAGUS HUMMUS

Very popular in the Middle East, falafels are often fried in copious amounts of oil. This baked version saves a bunch of calories but retains all the flavor. You could also use a store-bought hummus.   *Serves 6 to 12*   *V, F*

Falafel:

1½ cups dried chickpeas

1 medium onion, chopped

½ cup tightly packed chopped flat-leaf parsley

3 garlic cloves, minced

3 tablespoons flour

1½ teaspoons baking powder

1 teaspoon ground cumin

½ teaspoon ground coriander

½ teaspoon salt

¼ teaspoon cayenne pepper

juice of ½ lemon

Hummus:

½ bunch green asparagus (about ½ pound), woody ends trimmed and cut into 1-inch pieces

1 cup frozen shelled edamame

2 garlic cloves, minced

2 tablespoons tahini (sesame paste)

1 teaspoon grated lemon zest

juice of ½ lemon

a dash or two of cayenne pepper (optional)

¼ cup extra-virgin olive oil

salt and black pepper

For the Falafel: Place the chickpeas in a large bowl and add enough cold water to cover them by at least 2 inches. Let soak overnight or at least several hours.

Drain and rinse the chickpeas, and transfer to a food processor along with the remaining falafel ingredients. Process until the mixture is grainy but not a paste. You want a texture similar to bottled minced garlic. Refrigerate the mixture for at least 2 hours. This helps the falafels hold together during baking.

Preheat the oven to 350°F. Divide the chickpea mixture among 24 mini muffin cups, making sure to firmly pack each muffin mold to ensure they hold together during cooking. Bake until set and golden on top, about 20 minutes. Let cool for 5 minutes before unmolding.

For the Hummus: Bring a large pot of salted water to a boil and fill a large bowl with ice water. Add the asparagus to the pot, return the water to boil, and cook until the asparagus is tender, about 3 minutes. Using a slotted spoon, transfer the asparagus to the ice water and let sit for 5 minutes. This helps keep the asparagus bright green and prevents it from going mushy. Add the edamame to the pot of boiling water, return to a boil, and cook until the beans are tender, about 5 minutes. Drain and transfer the edamame to a food processor. Drain the asparagus well, pat dry with a paper towel, and add to the food processor along with the garlic, tahini, lemon zest, lemon juice, cayenne pepper, if using, and salt and black pepper to taste. Blend until the asparagus is broken down. With the processor running, pour in the olive oil through the feed tube and process until smooth and the asparagus is no longer fibrous, 1 to 2 minutes. Add more oil if needed to reach the desired consistency. Serve with the falafels.

PANCETTA CUPS WITH FIG JAM

Pancetta is Italian bacon that's cured with salt, but not smoked. Most well-stocked deli counters now carry it. Look for pancetta that comes in a cylinder (sausage) shape, which will make perfect-size rounds when sliced. But request that your pancetta is not sliced paper thin so it can be stuffed into the muffin molds without falling apart.   *Serves 6 to 12*   G

4 ounces chopped dried Mission figs (about 1 cup)

¾ cup apple cider

2 tablespoons honey

½ teaspoon ground cinnamon

1 tablespoon lemon juice

24 slices pancetta (not paper-thin)

In a medium saucepan over high heat, bring the figs and apple cider to a boil. Reduce the heat to medium-low and simmer, covered, for 15 minutes. Transfer the figs and cider to a blender or food processor along with the honey, cinnamon, and lemon juice, and puree until smooth.

Snugly fit the slices of pancetta into 24 mini muffin cups. It's OK if the pancetta does not cover the cups entirely. Place the tin in a cold oven, turn the heat to 400°F, and bake until crispy, about 12 minutes. Let cool for several minutes before carefully unmolding, then place the cups directly on a wire rack lined with a paper towel to cool completely. Fill the cooled pancetta cups with the fig jam.

Top: PANCETTA CUPS WITH FIG JAM, *page 56*
Bottom: BITTY BURGERS, *page 58*

BITTY BURGERS

If any appetizer in this book is going to impress, it's gotta be these darlings. Have all the components ready when the cooked meat comes out of the oven to make assembly a breeze and to ensure you're serving them warm. These tend to be two bites, so serve with cocktail napkins.   *Serves 12*   F

1 large egg

1 pound lean ground beef or other red meat

¼ cup bread crumbs

1 tablespoon grainy or Dijon mustard

2 teaspoons fresh thyme or 1 teaspoon dried thyme

½ teaspoon salt

½ cup shredded cheddar cheese (about 2 ounces)

4 whole-grain pocket pitas

½ cup roasted red pepper, sliced into 1-inch pieces

½ cup baby spinach or other green, sliced into 1-inch pieces

Preheat the oven to 375°F. In a large bowl, lightly beat the egg. Add the beef, bread crumbs, mustard, thyme, and salt. Mix gently with your hands. Divide the mixture among 24 mini muffin cups and bake until an internal temperature of 160°F is reached, about 12 minutes. Remove the pan from the oven, top each burger ball with cheese, and bake for 1 minute more. Let cool for about 5 minutes before unmolding.

Slice a pita in half and then run your knife along the insides of each half to separate the lower and upper parts of the pita to create four total pieces. Slice into 1 x 2-inch pieces. Repeat with the remaining pitas. To assemble, place each mini burger on a pita slice and top with roasted red pepper and spinach. Place another pita slice on top and press a toothpick through to the bottom.

PIZZA BITES WITH MARINARA SAUCE

These addictive little things are sure to be a star on the hors d'oeuvres table.
I've provided a simple yet highly flavorful recipe for marinara dipping
sauce, but store-bought will certainly do if you're in a time crunch.
Serves 6 to 12   F

Pizza Bites:

¾ cup whole wheat pastry flour or spelt flour

2 teaspoons fresh oregano or 1 teaspoon dried oregano

2 teaspoons fresh thyme or 1 teaspoon dried thyme

¾ teaspoon baking powder

¼ teaspoon salt

1 large egg

¾ cup low-fat milk

½ cup shredded cheddar cheese (about 2 ounces), preferably sharp

½ cup shredded mozzarella cheese (about 2 ounces)

¾ cup finely chopped pepperette or pepperoni, hot or mild

Marinara Sauce:

1 pound plum (Roma) tomatoes, quartered

4 garlic cloves, chopped

2 tablespoons balsamic vinegar

1 tablespoon fresh oregano or 1 teaspoon dried oregano

½ teaspoon salt

¼ teaspoon pepper

3 tablespoons extra-virgin olive oil

For the Pizza Bites: In a large bowl, stir together the flour, oregano, thyme, baking powder, and salt. In a second large bowl, lightly beat the egg. Stir in the milk, cheddar cheese, mozzarella cheese, and pepperette or pepperoni. Add the wet ingredients to dry and stir gently. Divide the mixture among 24 mini muffin cups and bake until puffed and golden, about 15 minutes.

For the Marinara Sauce: Place the tomatoes, garlic, vinegar, oregano, salt, and pepper in a blender or food processor and puree until smooth. Pour the mixture into a saucepan and stir in the olive oil. Bring to a boil over high heat, reduce the heat to low, and maintain a strong simmer until slightly thickened, about 30 minutes. Serve with the pizza bites.

PRETZEL ROUNDS WITH HONEY MUSTARD DIPPING SAUCE

If you're looking for a perfect nibble for the big game, both sports fans and non-enthusiasts alike will snatch up these pipsqueak pretzels.

Serves 6 to 12   V, F

Pretzel Bites:

¾ cup plus 2 tablespoons lukewarm water (105 to 115°F)

1 packet (2¼ teaspoons) active dry yeast

1 teaspoon coconut palm sugar or other granulated sugar

½ teaspoon salt

1 cup whole wheat flour (preferably not pastry)

1 cup all-purpose flour

2 tablespoons yellow cornmeal

2 tablespoons baking soda

1 large egg beaten with 1 tablespoon cold water, for egg wash

1 teaspoon coarse salt

Mustard Sauce:

½ cup low-fat plain yogurt

2 tablespoons yellow mustard

1 tablespoon honey

For the Pretzel Bites: In a large bowl, stir together the water, yeast, sugar, and salt. Let stand until the yeast has dissolved, about 5 minutes. Add the whole wheat flour, all-purpose flour, and cornmeal and stir until the dough begins to come together. If it's too crumbly, add an additional tablespoon of water. Place the dough on a floured work surface and knead until smooth and elastic, about 5 minutes. If an indentation remains in the dough when pressed with your finger, it's ready for rising. Place the dough in a large bowl with a little oil, turn to coat, and cover with a clean kitchen towel. Set aside in a warm, draft-free place until roughly doubled in size, about 1 hour.

Preheat the oven to 400°F. Divide the dough into 24 equal rounds. Fill a large saucepan one-quarter full of water, add the baking soda, and bring to a boil. Add half of the dough rounds to the water and boil for 1 minute. Using a slotted spoon to drain off any excess water, remove the boiled dough pieces. Repeat with remaining dough rounds. Place the rounds in 24 mini muffin cups, brush each with egg wash, and sprinkle the tops with coarse salt. Bake until golden brown on top, about 15 minutes. Let cool for several minutes before unmolding.

For the Mustard Sauce: Place the yogurt, mustard, and honey in a small bowl and whisk until combined. Serve with the pretzel bites.

MINTED AVOCADO CUPS

Crunchy wontons provide a nice contrast to the fresh-tasting, creamy avocado mixture. The filling doesn't store well, so try to whip it up as close to serving as possible.   *Serves 6 to 12*   *V*

24 wonton wrappers

grapeseed or canola oil, as needed

⅔ cup low-fat sour cream

juice of 1 lime

2 tablespoons finely chopped fresh mint

1 garlic clove, grated

¼ teaspoon salt

hot sauce or cayenne pepper

4 ripe avocados, diced

Preheat the oven to 375°F. Using a pastry brush, lightly coat both sides of the wonton wrappers with oil. Press the wrappers into 24 mini muffin cups, making sure the bottoms are as flat as possible. Bake until golden and crisp, 8 to 10 minutes, being careful not to burn them. Let cool for several minutes before unmolding.

In a large bowl, stir together the sour cream, lime juice, mint, garlic, salt, and hot sauce or cayenne pepper to taste. Gently stir in the avocado until coated. Divide the avocado mixture among the wonton cups and serve.

APPLE AND SAUSAGE MINI QUICHES

These delights hit the sweet, smoky, and savory taste notes. Look for puff pastry in the frozen food department of your grocer. Of course, if you have a cherished DIY pastry recipe, by all means use it. (I don't pretend to have the knack for making good puff pastry.) You can also find prerolled puff pastry at some grocers.   *Serves 6 to 12*

7 ounces (½ package) puff pastry, thawed

4 large eggs

½ cup cooked chorizo sausage, finely chopped

1 small apple, finely diced

2 ounces camembert or brie cheese, diced

2 teaspoons grainy or Dijon mustard

1 tablespoon fresh thyme

salt and pepper

Preheat the oven to 375°F. Grease 24 mini muffin cups with butter. On a lightly floured work surface, roll out the puff pastry into a 12-inch square. Cut 24 (2-inch) rounds using a cookie cutter, a ¼-cup measure, or similar object about the size of the top of a mini muffin cup. Carefully press the pastry rounds into the prepared muffin cups, making sure the bottoms are flat. Poke the bottoms with a fork to prevent puffing.

In a large bowl, lightly beat the eggs and stir in the sausage, apple, cheese, mustard, thyme, and salt and pepper to taste. Divide the mixture among the pastry cups and bake until the eggs are puffed and set, about 15 minutes. Let cool for several minutes before unmolding.

STARS OF THE SHOW: MAIN DISHES

With a little bit of creativity, it's easy to use your muffin tin to turn out all-star entrees. Several of the recipes in this chapter, such as lasagna and meatloaf, are classic main dishes, but with the unexpected sparkle of being round, not flat. I'm a big proponent of Meatless Mondays (and Tuesdays!) as way to reduce the burden that our heavy intake of animal protein is having on our health and the planet's, so I've included a number of mains that work within the spirit of this noble cause. Best of all, all these make for wonderful leftovers so you're set for another meal or two during a busy work week. When possible, I've imbued these recipes with as many good-for-you ingredients such as whole grains, lean proteins, and vegetables as possible. But I guess that's just the dietitian in me at work.

LASAGNA ROLLS

Most muffin tin lasagnas floating around the Web use wonton wrappers, but I think a more authentic and flavorful result comes from taking the extra effort to use lasagna noodles. When using a store-bought tomato sauce, I'll often jazz it up by blending it with mushrooms, red wine vinegar, red chili flakes, oregano, or other seasonings.   *Serves 6   V, F*

9 whole wheat lasagna noodles

2 cups store-bought pasta sauce or homemade (see page 84), divided

1½ cups reduced-fat ricotta cheese

4 ounces chopped spinach (about 3 cups)

1 cup shredded mozzarella cheese (about 4 ounces)

salt

torn fresh basil, to serve

grated Parmesan cheese, to serve

In a large pot of water, cook the lasagna noodles according to the package directions until al dente. Depending on the size of your pot, you may need to do this in batches. Divide half of the pasta sauce among 6 jumbo muffin cups. Lay the noodles on a flat work surface and spread the ricotta cheese over each one. Top the ricotta with the spinach, and tightly roll the noodles. Slice each roll in half and stuff three lasagna rounds into each of 6 jumbo muffin cups with the cut sides up. Sprinkle the tops with a dash of salt. Top with the remaining sauce and the mozzarella cheese.

Bake until the cheese is melted and bubbly, about 20 minutes. Let cool for several minutes before unmolding. As they cool, the lasagna rolls will meld together. To unmold, run a butter knife around the edges, place a flat object such as a cutting board on top of the tin and turn upside down. If desired, serve with torn basil, grated Parmesan cheese, and/or additional pasta sauce.

Top: LASAGNA ROLLS, *page 64*
Bottom: TURKEY POT PIES, *page 66*

TURKEY POT PIES

Wholesome and comforting, pot pies are sometimes unbeatable. This recipe would be a good way to use leftover holiday turkey.   *Serves 6   F*

2 tablespoons grapeseed or canola oil, divided

⅓ pound turkey breast or thigh meat, diced into small cubes

1 leek, thinly sliced, white and light green parts

1 celery rib, chopped

1 large carrot, chopped

2 cups chopped cremini mushrooms

2 garlic cloves, minced

2 tablespoons flour

1 teaspoon dried thyme

½ teaspoon salt

¼ teaspoon pepper

2 cups reduced-sodium chicken broth

⅓ cup frozen peas

7-ounces puff pastry (½ package), thawed

1 large egg beaten with 1 tablespoon water, for egg wash

Heat 1 tablespoon of the oil in a large saucepan over medium heat. Add the turkey and cook until no longer pink, about 6 minutes. Remove the turkey and rinse the pan. Then in the same pan add the remaining 1 tablespoon oil and cook the leeks, celery, and carrot, stirring occasionally, until softened, about 5 minutes. Add the mushrooms and garlic, and cook, stirring occasionally, until softened, about 3 minutes. Add the flour, thyme, salt, and pepper, and cook, stirring constantly, for 1 minute. Slowly pour in the broth, stirring and scraping up the browned bits at the bottom of the pan. Bring to a boil, reduce the heat to low, and simmer for 10 minutes. Stir in the cooked turkey and the peas. Turn off the heat.

Preheat the oven to 400°F. On a lightly floured work surface, roll out the puff pastry into a 12-inch square. Using a knife or pizza wheel, cut the pastry into 12 rectangular pieces by slicing 4 vertical rows and 3 horizontal rows. Fit the rectangles into 12 medium muffin cups, making sure there is some overhang. Divide the turkey mixture among the muffin cups. Pull in all four points of each crust over the filling so they meet in the middle, forming individual pot pies. Brush each pie with the egg wash and bake until crisp and deeply golden, about 20 minutes. Let cool for several minutes before umolding and serving.

MEATLOAVES WITH CHIMICHURRI SAUCE

The best thing about individual meatloaves is they cook in less than half the time it takes regular meatloaf prepared in a loaf pan to cook. Chipotle chile pepper in adobo sauce adds a hint of smoky heat and can be found in the Latin section of better grocers. *Serves 6* *F*

Chimichurri Sauce:

1½ cups flat-leaf parsley, tightly packed

2 tablespoons fresh oregano, tightly packed

2 garlic cloves, chopped

⅓ cup extra-virgin olive oil

2 tablespoons red wine vinegar

juice of ½ lemon

½ teaspoon red pepper flakes

salt and pepper

Meatloaf:

2 shallots, finely chopped

2 garlic cloves, minced

1 medium carrot, peeled and shredded

⅓ cup quick-cook rolled oats (not instant) or bread crumbs

1 egg, lightly beaten

1 teaspoon ground cumin

2 tablespoons ketchup or 1 tablespoon tomato paste

2 teaspoons Worcestershire sauce

½ cup chopped sun-dried tomatoes

1 tablespoon minced chipotle chile in adobo sauce (optional)

¼ teaspoon ground nutmeg

¼ teaspoon salt

¼ teaspoon pepper

1 pound lean ground red meat, such as beef or bison

For the Chimichurri Sauce: Place the parsley, oregano, and garlic in the bowl of a food processor. Pulse several times to finely chop the herbs. Add the olive oil, red wine vinegar, lemon juice, red pepper flakes, and salt and pepper to taste; pulse until combined.

For the Meatloaf: Preheat the oven to 375°F. In a large bowl, use a fork to mix together the shallots, garlic, carrot, oats or bread crumbs, egg, cumin, ketchup or tomato paste, Worcestershire sauce, sun-dried tomatoes, chipotle chile, if using, nutmeg, salt, and pepper. Gently mix in the ground meat. Divide the mixture among 12 medium muffin cups and bake until an internal temperature of 160°F is reached, about 25 minutes. Serve with chimichurri sauce.

EGGPLANT PARMESAN

Try this recipe and you can bid adieu to heavy, greasy, uninspiring eggplant Parmesan.   *Serves 6   V*

1½ cups canned crushed fire-roasted tomatoes

⅓ cup fresh basil leaves, plus more for garnish

2 garlic cloves, minced

1 tablespoon red wine vinegar

¼ teaspoon red pepper flakes

1 large egg

1 tablespoon water

1 cup panko (Japanese-style) bread crumbs

1 teaspoon dried oregano

½ cup grated Parmesan or Parmigiano-Reggiano cheese (about 2 ounces), divided

2 medium eggplants (about 1 pound)

1½ cups shredded regular or part-skim mozzarella (about 6 ounces)

1 cup sliced rapini (broccoli rabe)

salt and pepper

Preheat the oven to 375°F. Line a baking sheet with parchment paper or a silicone baking mat. In a blender or food processor, puree the tomatoes, basil, garlic, red wine vinegar, red pepper flakes, and salt to taste; set aside.

In a small bowl, lightly the beat egg with the water. In a shallow container, combine the panko bread crumbs, oregano, and ¼ cup of the Parmesan or Parmigiano-Reggiano cheese, and season with salt and pepper. Slice the eggplants into 18 rounds ¼ inch thick. If needed, trim the rounds so the slices fit into the jumbo muffin cups. One at a time, dip the eggplant rounds in the egg mixture, then dredge in the panko mixture, pressing gently to adhere. Place the eggplant on the prepared baking sheet and bake until golden, about 30 minutes, flipping the slices and rotating the baking sheet after 15 minutes.

To assemble, place a slice of toasted eggplant in each of 6 jumbo muffin cups. Top each with about 1½ tablespoons of the tomato sauce and 1½ tablespoons of the mozzarella. Top with a sprinkle of the rapini. Place another eggplant slice on top and top with about 1½ tablespoons of the tomato sauce and 1½ tablespoons of the mozzarella, and evenly sprinkle the remaining rapini among the cups. Place the remaining eggplant slices on top and evenly top with the remaining tomato sauce, remaining mozzarella, and the remaining ¼ cup Parmesan or Parmigiano-Reggiano cheese. Bake until the cheese melts, about 10 minutes. Let cool for a few minutes before unmolding. Serve garnished with fresh basil.

Top: EGGPLANT PARMESAN, *page 68*
Bottom: MINI MACARONI AND CHEESE, *page 70*

MINI MACARONI AND CHEESE

Sure, mac 'n' cheese is pure comfort food. But too often it's a calorie landmine courtesy of the gooey cheese, which is why making individual servings in a muffin tin is the perfect way to control portions. Kids are sure to love this reinvention bejeweled with crunchy panko crumbs. *Serves 4   V, F*

8 ounces whole-grain macaroni (elbow) pasta

1½ cups shredded cheddar cheese (about 6 ounces)

½ cup plus 2 tablespoons grated Parmesan cheese (about 2½ ounces), divided

2 large eggs

¾ cup low-fat milk

⅓ cup plain low-fat yogurt, preferably Greek-style

½ cup chopped sun-dried tomatoes

2 tablespoons chopped chives

¼ teaspoon cayenne pepper (optional)

¼ teaspoon ground nutmeg

1 tablespoon grainy or Dijon mustard

¼ teaspoon salt

¼ teaspoon black pepper

2 tablespoons unsalted butter

¾ cup panko (Japanese-style) bread crumbs

Cook the macaroni according to the package instructions until al dente. Preheat the oven to 375°F. Drain the pasta, return it to the pot, and stir in the cheddar cheese and ½ cup of the Parmesan cheese. In a medium bowl, lightly beat the eggs and stir in the milk and yogurt. Add the egg mixture to the pasta mixture along with the sun-dried tomatoes, chives, cayenne, if using, nutmeg, mustard, salt, and pepper and mix well. Divide the mixture among 12 medium muffin cups. Heat the butter in a medium skillet over medium heat. Stir in the bread crumbs and cook until browned, stirring regularly. Stir the remaining 2 tablespoons Parmesan cheese into the toasted bread crumbs, sprinkle over the pasta mixture, and bake until set, about 15 minutes. Let cool for 5 minutes before unmolding.

PIZZA DOUGH

On the following pages you'll find a trio of ways to jazz up pizza night or a potluck. Consider getting the kids involved in the assembly of the pizza cups. If you want to serve up more than one flavor, you could even use half of the dough for one recipe and the other half for another. Certainly you can use store-bought pizza dough to save time, but I often find the results are better when you make your own. And this no-fuss crust recipe doesn't require a culinary arts degree to master. *Serves 6, makes enough for 12 muffin-size pizzas*

¾ cup plus 2 tablespoons lukewarm water (105 to 115°F)

1 packet (2¼ teaspoons) active dry yeast

1 teaspoon coconut palm sugar or other granulated sugar

½ teaspoon salt

1 cup whole wheat flour (preferably not pastry)

1 cup all-purpose flour or bread flour

2 tablespoons yellow cornmeal

In a large bowl, stir together the water, yeast, sugar, and salt. Let stand until the yeast has dissolved, about 5 minutes. Add the whole wheat flour, all-purpose or bread flour, and cornmeal to the bowl and mix until the dough begins to come together. If it's too crumbly, add more water 1 tablespoon at a time until it holds together. (The dough should look somewhat dry). Place the dough on a floured work surface and knead until smooth and elastic, about 5 minutes. If an indentation remains in the dough when pressed with your finger, it's ready for rising. Place the dough in a bowl with a little oil, turn to coat, and cover with a clean kitchen towel. Set aside in a warm, draft-free place until roughly doubled in size, about 1 hour.

SPINACH PESTO—BACON PIZZA

Serves 6 *F*

2 cups packed spinach

⅓ cup grated Parmesan cheese (about 2 ounces)

¼ cup coarsely chopped walnuts or pine nuts

2 cloves garlic, chopped

juice of ½ lemon

¼ cup extra-virgin olive oil

1 recipe Pizza Dough (page 71)

½ pound cooked Canadian bacon, diced (about 1 cup)

1 cup sliced cherry tomatoes

¾ cup shredded white cheddar cheese (about 2 ounces)

salt

In a food processor, pulse together the spinach, Parmesan cheese, walnuts or pine nuts, garlic, lemon juice, and salt to taste until the spinach is finely chopped. With the motor running, add the olive oil in a thin stream through the feed tube and blend until well combined.

Divide the pizza dough into 12 equal balls. Flatten one ball into a 6-inch round and stuff into a medium muffin cup. Repeat with the remaining rounds. Spread pesto in the bottom of the dough cups and top with the bacon, tomatoes, and white cheddar cheese. Bake until the crust is golden and crisp, about 15 minutes. Let cool for several minutes before unmolding. Garnish with additional pesto.

CHICKEN ITALIANO PIZZA

Serves 6   F

½ pound cooked boneless chicken breast or thigh meat, diced (about 1 cup)

1 cup marinara sauce, store-bought or homemade (see page 59)

2 garlic cloves, minced

⅓ cup sliced black olives

⅓ cup torn fresh basil, plus more for garnish

¼ teaspoon red pepper flakes (optional)

1 cup shredded mozzarella (about 4 ounces), divided

1 recipe Pizza Dough (page 71)

salt and pepper

Preheat the oven to 400°F. In a large bowl, stir together the chicken, marinara sauce, garlic, olives, basil, red pepper flakes, if using, ½ cup of the mozzarella, and salt and pepper to taste. Divide the pizza dough into 12 equal balls. Flatten one ball into a 6-inch round and stuff into a medium muffin cup. Repeat with the remaining rounds. Divide the chicken mixture among the dough cups and top with the remaining mozzarella. Bake until the crust is golden and crisp, about 15 minutes. Let cool for several minutes before unmolding, and garnish with additional basil.

BUTTERNUT SQUASH AND CARAMELIZED ONION PIZZA
Serves 6   V, F

1 tablespoon unsalted butter

1 large sweet onion, thinly sliced

1 tablespoon coconut palm sugar or brown sugar

1 teaspoon balsamic vinegar

½ pound butternut squash, cubed (you can also use frozen winter squash)

1 tablespoon chopped fresh sage or 1 teaspoon dried sage

¼ teaspoon salt

¼ teaspoon pepper

1 recipe Pizza Dough (page 71)

1 cup chopped arugula

⅔ cup diced roasted red pepper

¾ cup crumbled semisoft goat cheese (about 3 ounces)

Melt the butter in a large saucepan or skillet over medium heat. Add the onion and cook until translucent, 4 to 5 minutes. Stir in the sugar and balsamic vinegar. Reduce the heat to medium-low, cover, and cook, stirring occasionally, until the onion is very soft and caramelized, about 30 minutes.

Roast, steam, or boil the squash until tender. Transfer to a medium bowl, mash with a fork or potato masher, and mix in the sage, salt, and pepper.

Preheat the oven to 400°F. Divide the pizza dough into 12 equal balls. Flatten one ball into a 6-inch round and stuff into a medium muffin cup. Repeat with the remaining rounds. Spread butternut puree in the bottoms of the dough cups and top with arugula, roasted red pepper, and goat cheese. Bake until the crust is golden and crisp, about 15 minutes. Let cool for several minutes before unmolding. Serve with the caramelized onion.

Top: BUTTERNUT SQUASH AND CARAMELIZED ONION PIZZA, *page 74*

Bottom:: CURRY TUNA NOODLE CASSEROLE, *page 76*

CURRY TUNA NOODLE CASSEROLE

Using whole-grain penne instead of nutritionally lackluster egg noodles and real mushrooms over canned cream-of-mushroom soup gives these individual tuna casseroles a healthy lift.   *Serves 6   V, G*

4 ounces brown rice penne (about 1½ cups)

1 tablespoon unsalted butter

2 cups diced cremini mushrooms

1 cup diced red bell pepper

1 shallot or small onion, finely diced

½ cup frozen peas

2 teaspoons curry powder

1 tablespoon fresh thyme or 1 teaspoon dried thyme

2 large eggs

2 (5-ounce) cans white albacore tuna, flaked

1½ cups shredded white cheddar cheese (about 6 ounces), divided

½ cup low-fat milk

juice of ½ lemon

grated Parmesan cheese, for garnish (optional)

salt and pepper

Cook the pasta according to package directions until al dente. Drain and set aside.

Preheat oven to 375°F. Melt the butter in a skillet over medium heat. Add the mushrooms, bell pepper, and shallot or onion; cook for 5 minutes. Add the peas, curry powder, thyme, and salt and pepper to taste; heat until the peas are tender, about 1 minute.

In a large bowl, lightly beat the eggs. Stir in the cooked pasta, cooked vegetable mixture, tuna, 1 cup of the white cheddar cheese, and the milk and lemon juice. Divide the mixture among 6 jumbo muffin cups, making sure the contents are tightly packed. Top with the remaining ½ cup white cheddar cheese and bake until set and golden on top, about 25 minutes. Let cool for several minutes before unmolding. Garnish with Parmesan cheese, if desired.

STEAK BURRITO BOWLS

Home-style burritos in a toasty bowl. Mexican food lovers rejoice! If you find your tortillas are too big to fit properly in the muffin molds, use kitchen shears to cut away about an inch around the edges.   *Serves 6*

1 tablespoon grapeseed or canola oil

8 ounces steak, sliced into ½-inch cubes

1 cup cooked brown rice

1 cup canned (drained and rinsed) or cooked dried black beans

1 small red bell pepper, finely chopped

2 green onions, white and green parts, thinly sliced

1 ripe avocado, diced

juice of ½ lime

¾ cup prepared tomato salsa, mild or hot

12 (6-inch) whole wheat tortillas

2 cups shredded sharp cheddar cheese (about 8 ounces)

salt and pepper

Preheat the oven to 375°F. Heat a wok or skillet over medium-high heat. Add the oil, swirl to coat the pan, and add the steak. Cook, stirring occasionally, until browned, 2 to 3 minutes. In a large bowl, combine the steak, rice, beans, bell pepper, green onions, avocado, lime juice, and salt and pepper to taste. Stir in the salsa. Stuff the tortillas into 12 jumbo muffin cups. Distribute half of the cheddar cheese in the bottom of the tortilla cups, and top with the steak mixture and the remaining cheese. Bake until the tortillas have turned crispy, about 10 minutes. Let cool for several minutes before unmolding.

TACO CUPS

Here's a fun twist for taco night. Forget the table manners; just pick these up and devour.   *Serves 6   V, G*

6 (5-inch) corn tortillas

1 tablespoon grapeseed or canola oil, plus more for brushing the tortillas

½ teaspoon chili powder

½ teaspoon ground cumin

½ teaspoon onion powder

½ teaspoon garlic powder

½ teaspoon salt

¼ teaspoon pepper

¼ teaspoon paprika

1 teaspoon dried oregano

½ pound lean ground red meat, such as beef or bison

½ pound cremini mushrooms, finely chopped

1 medium red bell pepper, diced

½ medium yellow onion, diced

⅔ cup shredded Monterey Jack cheese

⅔ cup shredded sharp cheddar cheese

½ cup sliced cherry tomatoes

⅓ cup chopped fresh cilantro

Heat the tortillas one at a time in a dry skillet over medium-high heat until soft and pliable, 15 to 20 seconds per side. Or, stack the tortillas and microwave on high power uncovered until warm and flexible, about 25 seconds. Brush both sides of the warm tortillas with oil. With the bottom of a glass, gently press the tortillas into 6 jumbo muffin cups. Don't worry if some of the tortilla folds inward.

Preheat the oven to 375°F. In a small bowl, stir together the chili powder, cumin, onion powder, garlic powder, salt, pepper, paprika, and oregano. Heat 1 tablespoon of the oil in a large skillet over medium heat. Add the spice mixture and the ground meat, mushrooms, bell pepper, and onion. Cook until the meat is no longer red and the mushrooms have softened, stirring occasionally, about 7 minutes. In a small bowl, combine the Monterey Jack cheese and the cheddar cheese. Add a 1-tablespoon layer of cheese to the bottom of each tortilla cup and evenly top with the meat mixture. Sprinkle the remaining cheese on top and bake until the tortillas begin to brown on the edges and the cheese is nicely melted, about 15 minutes. Serve topped with cherry tomatoes and cilantro.

Top: TACO CUPS, *page 78*
Bottom: FISH TACOS, *page 80*

FISH TACOS

Cast your line for this weeknight-friendly, fast, and fun twist on tacos. The smoky yogurt sauce and tropical mango flavor take them from OK to oh, yeah!   *Serves 6   G*

6 (5-inch) corn tortillas

grapeseed or canola oil, as needed

1½ cups shredded cabbage or lettuce

¾ pound tilapia or catfish

1 teaspoon ground cumin

½ teaspoon salt

¼ teaspoon pepper

½ teaspoon paprika

grated zest of 1 lime

1 cup cubed mango (about 1 medium)

1 ripe avocado, cubed

⅓ cup chopped fresh cilantro

2 green onions, green and white parts, thinly sliced

juice of 1 lime, divided

½ cup plain yogurt, preferably Greek-style

1 to 2 teaspoons finely chopped canned chipotle chile pepper in adobo sauce

Heat the tortillas one at a time in a dry skillet over medium-high heat until soft and pliable, 15 to 20 seconds per side. Or, stack the tortillas and microwave on high power uncovered until warm and flexible, about 25 seconds. Brush both sides of the warm tortillas with oil. With the bottom of a glass, gently press the tortillas into 6 jumbo muffin cups. Don't worry if some of the tortilla folds inward.

Preheat the oven to 375°F. Divide the cabbage or lettuce among the tortilla cups. Wash the fish with cold water and pat dry with a paper towel. Slice the fish into 1-inch cubes and place in a medium bowl. In a small bowl, stir together the cumin, salt, pepper, paprika, and lime zest. Sprinkle the spice mixture over the fish and toss to coat. Divide the fish among the tortilla cups and bake until the fish is cooked through, about 15 minutes.

In a small bowl, toss together the mango, avocado, cilantro, green onions, juice of ½ lime, and salt to taste. In a second small bowl, stir together the yogurt, chipotle chile, and the remaining lime juice. Serve the fish tacos topped with the mango salsa and a dollop of yogurt sauce.

SALMON CAKES WITH GRILLED PEACH SALSA

Versatile canned salmon is a natural fit for muffin tin entree creations. If possible, splurge and use canned salmon from a smaller-scale company such as Wild Planet (www.wildplanetfoods.com) that employs sustainable fishing practices and, frankly, offers a much more flavorful product. *Serves 4*

Salsa:

4 medium peaches, sliced in half and pitted

2 medium red bell peppers

grapeseed or canola oil, as needed

½ red onion, finely diced

1 jalapeño pepper, seeded and minced

⅓ cup chopped fresh cilantro

⅓ cup chopped fresh mint

juice of ½ lime

1 teaspoon grated orange zest

Salmon Cakes:

2 (6-ounce) cans pink or sockeye salmon, drained

1 medium carrot, peeled and shredded

1 shallot, finely chopped

½ cup bread crumbs

½ cup low-fat milk

2 large eggs, lightly beaten

juice of 1 lemon

2 tablespoons chopped fresh tarragon

1 teaspoon fennel seeds, preferably ground in a mortar and pestle

¾ teaspoon paprika, preferably smoked

¼ teaspoon salt

¼ teaspoon pepper

For the Salsa: Preheat a grill to medium. Brush the peaches and bell peppers with oil. Grill the peaches until slightly charred, about 4 minutes per side. Grill the red peppers until slightly charred all over, turning about every 2 minutes. Let cool. In a medium bowl, toss together the red onion, jalapeño, cilantro, mint, lime juice, and orange zest. Remove the skin from the peaches. Chop the peaches and red pepper, and stir into the onion mixture.

For the Salmon Cakes: Preheat the oven to 350°F. In a large bowl, flake the salmon with a fork. Using a fork, mix in the carrot, shallot, bread crumbs, milk, eggs, lemon juice, tarragon, fennel seeds, paprika, salt, and pepper. Divide the mixture among 10 medium muffin cups and pack down gently with the back of a spoon. Bake until slightly browned on top and set, about 25 minutes. Let the cakes rest for several minutes before unmolding. Serve with the peach salsa.

CRAB CAKES WITH CORN-TOMATO RELISH

These delightful crab cakes are considerably lighter than the fried version. One cup frozen corn kernels can be used in place of fresh.   *Serves 6*

Crab Cakes:

2 large eggs

1 cup panko (Japanese-style) bread crumbs

½ red bell pepper, finely chopped

1 celery rib, finely chopped

2 garlic cloves, minced

3 tablespoons finely chopped chives

2 teaspoons grainy or Dijon mustard

1 teaspoon grated lemon zest

juice of ½ lemon

several dashes of hot sauce such as Sriracha or ¼ teaspoon cayenne pepper

¼ cup reduced-fat sour cream

¼ teaspoon salt

¼ teaspoon black pepper

2 (5-ounce) cans chunk crabmeat or about 10 ounces fresh lump crabmeat

Corn Relish:

2 ears corn

grapeseed or canola oil, as needed

1 red bell pepper, diced

1 cup cherry tomatoes, quartered

1 avocado, diced

1 jalapeño pepper, seeded and finely diced

2 green onions, green and white parts, sliced

2 tablespoons red wine vinegar

juice of ½ lime

⅓ cup roughly chopped cilantro

For the Crab Cakes: Preheat the oven to 375°F. In a large bowl, lightly beat the eggs. Stir in the bread crumbs, bell pepper, celery, garlic, chives, mustard, lemon zest, lemon juice, hot sauce or cayenne pepper, sour cream, salt, and black pepper. Gently fold in the crabmeat and then divide the mixture among 12 medium muffin cups. Bake until golden and set, about 25 minutes. Let cool for several minutes before unmolding.

For the Corn Relish: Preheat a grill to medium. Remove the husks from the corn and brush the kernels with oil. Grill until the kernels are tender and slightly charred, turning the corn several times during grilling. Let cool and slice off the kernels into a bowl. Or, slice off the raw corn kernels and sauté in 1 tablespoon oil in a large skillet over medium heat until tender. Add the bell pepper, tomatoes, avocado, jalapeño, green onions, red wine vinegar, lime juice, and cilantro to the bowl and toss. Serve the crab cakes with the corn salsa.

Top: CRAB CAKES WITH CORN-TOMATO RELISH, *page 82*
Bottom: CHICKEN-RICE CABBAGE ROLLS, *page 84*

CHICKEN-RICE CABBAGE ROLLS

The mélange of rice, poultry, cheese, and an easy-peasy fresh tomato sauce team up to deliver a big time flavor punch.   *Serves 6   G, F*

Cabbage Rolls:

¾ cup Wehani rice or other brown rice

1½ cups water

1 tablespoon grapeseed or canola oil

1 pound ground chicken or turkey breast

1 large onion, diced

1 medium carrot, peeled and shredded

3 garlic cloves, minced

1 teaspoon dried thyme or oregano

¼ teaspoon salt

¼ teaspoon pepper

1½ cups shredded mozzarella cheese (about 6 ounces)

12 savoy cabbage leaves

Sauce:

5 plum (Roma) tomatoes

3 green onions, green and white parts, sliced

3 garlic cloves, minced

2 tablespoons red wine vinegar

⅓ cup tightly packed chopped fresh basil leaves

2 tablespoons fresh oregano or 1 teaspoon dried oregano

¼ teaspoon red pepper flakes

salt and pepper

For the Cabbage Rolls: Bring the rice and water to a boil in a medium saucepan over high heat. Reduce the heat to low and simmer, covered, until the rice is tender, about 30 minutes.

Meanwhile, heat the oil in a large skillet over medium heat. Add the chicken or turkey, onion, carrot, garlic, thyme, salt, and pepper. Cook until the chicken or turkey is browned throughout, then carefully drain away any excess liquid. Stir in the cooked rice and the mozzarella cheese.

Preheat the oven to 400°F. Bring a large pot of water to a boil and fill a large bowl with ice water. In batches, blanch the cabbage leaves in the hot water for 1 to 2 minutes to soften slightly and then plunge into the ice water. Drain, and slice off the tough lower spine of each cabbage leaf. Press the cabbage leaves into 12 medium muffin cups and fill each cup with the chicken or turkey mixture. Fold over the tops of the leaves to seal. Bake for about 20 minutes, being careful not to burn the leaves. While the rolls bake, prepare the sauce. When the rolls are done, let cool for about 5 minutes, and invert to unmold.

For the Sauce: Combine all the ingredients in a blender or food processor and pulse several times until well combined but still slightly chunky. Transfer the sauce to a medium saucepan over medium heat until hot. Serve over the cabbage rolls.

WILD RICE CABBAGE ROLLS

Wild rice and shiitake mushrooms give these meat-free cabbage rolls an earthy taste, while brie cheese provides ooey-gooey goodness. If you're like me and lack the finesse to properly roll cabbage leaves, making cabbage rolls in a muffin tin removes any angst. You'll want to use the inner, more delicate leaves, as the most outer ones will be too tough to properly fit into the muffin cups.   *Serves 6   V, G, F*

¾ cup wild rice

2 cups water

½ cup coarsely chopped walnuts

2 celery ribs, sliced thinly

1 cup sliced shiitake mushrooms

2 tablespoons fresh thyme

6 to 8 ounces brie cheese, diced

12 savoy cabbage leaves

salt and pepper

Bring the wild rice and water to a boil in a medium saucepan over high heat. Reduce the heat to low and simmer, covered, until the rice is tender, about 40 minutes. Drain the rice and add to a large bowl along with the walnuts, celery, mushrooms, thyme, brie, and salt and pepper to taste.

Preheat the oven to 400°F. Bring a large pot of water to a boil and fill a large bowl with ice water. In batches, blanch the cabbage leaves in the hot water for 1 to 2 minutes to soften slightly and then plunge into the ice water. Drain, and slice off the tough lower spine of each cabbage leaf. Press the cabbage leaves into 12 medium muffin cups, making sure a generous amount of leaf hangs over the sides. Fill each cup with the wild rice mixture. Fold over the tops of the leaves to seal. Bake for about 20 minutes, being careful not to burn the leaves. Let cool for about 5 minutes, then place a flat object such as a cutting board over the muffin tin and invert to unmold.

SWEET-AND-SOUR TOFU EGG ROLLS

This is very different from take-out sweet and sour. Low-fat tofu replaces deep-fried chicken and the sauce tastes much lighter and fresher than the mystery neon goop often served at restaurants.   *Serves 6   V*

⅓ cup reduced-sodium vegetable broth

1 tablespoon soy sauce or tamari

2 teaspoons toasted sesame oil

2 tablespoons seasoned rice vinegar

2 tablespoons ketchup

1 tablespoon coconut palm sugar or other granulated sugar

¼ cup plus 2 teaspoons cornstarch, divided

1 large egg white

1 tablespoon water

3 tablespoons coconut oil or other oil, divided

1 block firm tofu (about 12 ounces), cut into ¼-inch cubes

1 small green bell pepper, chopped

1 small red bell pepper, chopped

2 green onions, green and white parts, sliced

2 garlic cloves, minced

1 tablespoon minced ginger

1 cup cubed pineapple

12 egg roll wraps

salt

To make the sauce, in a small bowl, whisk together the vegetable broth, soy sauce or tamari, sesame oil, rice vinegar, ketchup, sugar, 2 teaspoons of the cornstarch, and salt to taste. Set aside. In a large bowl, whisk together the egg white and water. Add the tofu cubes and toss to coat. Stir in the remaining ¼ cup cornstarch and mix well.

Heat a wok or large skillet over medium-high heat. Add 2 tablespoons of the oil, swirl to coat the pan, and add the tofu. Cook until golden on all sides, about 6 minutes. Remove from the pan and set aside. Add the remaining 1 tablespoon oil to the pan, swirl to coat, and add the green and red bell pepper, green onions, garlic, and ginger. Cook until the peppers are tender, about 1 minute, stirring often. Pour in the sauce and cook until slightly thickened, about 30 seconds. Add the tofu and pineapple, and cook for 2 minutes, stirring often. Remove the pan from the heat.

Preheat the oven to 375°F. Press the egg roll wraps into 12 medium muffin cups. Fill each egg roll cup with the tofu mixture, fold over the tops to seal, and brush with oil. Bake until golden and crisp, about 15 minutes. Let cool for a few minutes before unmolding. Serve warm.

Top: SWEET-AND-SOUR TOFU EGG ROLLS, *page 86*
Bottom: PORK CAKES WITH APPLE-PLUM CHUTNEY, *page 88*

PORK CAKES WITH APPLE-PLUM CHUTNEY

Pork and apple is a classic combination that's hard to beat. The sweet apple chutney gussied up with dried plums just might be the star of the show here. The flavors of the pork cakes actually get better after a day or two. Use gluten-free oats as a binder if needed.   *Serves 6   F*

Chutney:

3 medium red apples, diced

1 cup chopped dried plums (prunes)

2 tablespoons coconut palm sugar or other granulated sugar

1 teaspoon brown mustard seeds (optional)

½ teaspoon ground cinnamon

¼ teaspoon ground cloves

1 teaspoon grated lemon zest

Pork Cakes:

1 large egg

1 shallot, finely chopped

2 garlic cloves, finely diced

1 jalapeño pepper, seeded and finely diced

1 tablespoon fresh sage or 1 teaspoon dried sage

2 teaspoons grainy or Dijon mustard

1 teaspoon ground cumin

⅓ cup bread crumbs or quick-cook rolled oats (not instant)

¼ teaspoon salt

¼ teaspoon pepper

1 pound lean ground pork

For the Chutney: Combine all the ingredients in a medium saucepan. Heat over medium heat until the apples begin to sizzle, then reduce the heat to medium-low and cook, covered, until the apples have softened and begun to break down, about 15 minutes.

For the Pork Cakes: Preheat the oven to 375°F. In a large bowl, lightly beat the egg. Mix in the shallot, garlic, jalapeño, sage, mustard, cumin, bread crumbs or oats, salt, and pepper. Gently mix in the ground pork until well combined. Divide the mixture among 12 medium muffin cups and bake until an internal temperature of 160°F is reached, about 25 minutes. Let cool for several minutes before unmolding. Serve with the apple-plum chutney.

BEAN LOAVES WITH TOMATO JAM

This vegan version of an American classic has a texture that's very similar to its meat-containing brethren. Give it a try on vegetarians and meat eaters   *Serves 6   V, F*

Tomato Jam:

1 pound plum (Roma) tomatoes (about 4)

2 tablespoons coconut palm sugar or other granulated sugar

1 tablespoon lemon juice

1 teaspoon paprika, preferably smoked

½ teaspoon salt

¼ teaspoon pepper

Bean Loaf:

1 cup quick-cook rolled oats (not instant)

1 small onion, finely diced

2 cloves garlic, chopped

½ cup sunflower seeds

1 (15-ounce) can chickpeas, drained and rinsed

1 (15-ounce) can pinto beans, drained and rinsed

1 tablespoon tomato paste

1 teaspoon ground cumin

1 teaspoon dried thyme

½ teaspoon chili powder

salt and pepper

For the Tomato Jam: Using a sharp knife, slice a shallow X into the bottom of each tomato. Fill a medium saucepan about halfway with water and bring to a boil. Drop the tomatoes into the boiling water for about 15 seconds and remove with a slotted spoon. When cool enough to handle, peel back the skin from the tomatoes, starting at the points created by the X. Slice in half, remove the seeds, and chop.

Combine the tomatoes and sugar in a medium saucepan. Let stand at room temperature for 10 minutes. Bring to a boil over high heat, then reduce the heat to low and simmer for 15 minutes, stirring often. Stir in the lemon juice, paprika, salt, and pepper. Cook until thickened, about 10 minutes.

For the Bean Loaf: Preheat the oven to 375°F. In a food processor, process the oats until broken down and powdery. Add the onion, garlic, and sunflower seeds and pulse until well combined. Add the chickpeas, pinto beans, tomato paste, cumin, thyme, chili powder, and salt and pepper to taste. Blend until a thick paste forms, making sure to leave a little bit of texture. Divide the mixture among 12 medium muffin cups and bake for 20 minutes. Let cool for several minutes before unmolding. Serve topped with warm tomato jam.

SWEET POTATO SHEPHERD'S PIE

Shepherd's pie has jumped out of the casserole dish and into the muffin tin. Replacing the white spud topping with sweet potato adds earthy sweetness and a splash of color. These are actually even better after a day or two sitting in the fridge. *Serves 6*   F

2 medium sweet potatoes, peeled and diced

1 tablespoon unsalted butter

¼ teaspoon ground nutmeg

2 tablespoons flour

1 tablespoon grapeseed or canola oil

1 small onion, finely diced

1 medium carrot, finely chopped

1 medium turnip, finely chopped

3 garlic cloves, minced

½ cup frozen corn kernels

⅔ pound ground turkey breast or chicken breast

½ cup bread crumbs

2 tablespoons tomato paste

2 teaspoons grainy mustard or Dijon mustard

1 large whole egg, lightly beaten

1 large egg white

1 tablespoon fresh thyme or 1 teaspoon dried thyme

¼ teaspoon salt

¼ teaspoon pepper

½ cup grated Parmesan cheese (about 2 ounces)

Steam or boil the sweet potatoes until very tender. Transfer to a medium bowl and mash with the butter, nutmeg, and flour; set aside. Heat the oil in a large skillet over medium heat. Cook the onion, carrot, turnip, and garlic until the vegetables are tender, about 8 minutes. Stir in the corn and cook until the corn is tender, about 1 minute.

Preheat the oven to 350°F. In a large bowl, mix together the turkey or chicken, cooked vegetables, bread crumbs, tomato paste, mustard, whole egg, egg white, thyme, salt, and pepper. Divide the mixture among 12 medium muffin cups. Spread the sweet potato mixture over the meat and top with the Parmesan cheese. Bake until set, about 25 minutes. Let cool for several minutes before unmolding.

Top: SWEET POTATO SHEPHERD'S PIE, *page 90*
Bottom: BROCCOLI-MUSHROOM FRITTATAS, *page 92*

BROCCOLI-MUSHROOM FRITTATAS

A frittata, a flat omelet as it's known in Italy, can be puffed up by swapping out the skillet for a muffin tin. What I love most about frittatas is that the ingredient possibilities are almost limitless. For a boost of protein, you could sneak in cooked chicken, diced anchovies, or your favorite sausage. There are countless other vegetable and cheese options.   *Serves 5*   *V, G*

1 tablespoon grapeseed or canola oil

3 cups chopped broccoli florets

½ cup diced broccoli stems, tough outer skin peeled off

2 cups sliced mushrooms

1 shallot, chopped

2 garlic cloves, minced

4 large whole eggs

3 egg whites

1 cup grated Gruyère or other Swiss-style hard cheese (about 4 ounces)

juice of ½ lemon

1 tablespoon fresh thyme or 1 teaspoon dried thyme

2 teaspoons grainy or Dijon mustard

¼ teaspoon red pepper flakes

¼ teaspoon salt

¼ teaspoon pepper

Preheat the oven to 375°F. Heat the oil in a large skillet over medium heat. Add the broccoli florets, broccoli stems, mushrooms, shallot, and garlic, and cook until the vegetables have softened, about 5 minutes. In a large bowl, beat together the whole eggs, egg whites, cheese, lemon juice, thyme, mustard, red pepper flakes, salt, and pepper. Stir in the broccoli mixture. Divide the mixture among 10 medium muffin cups and bake until the eggs have set, about 20 minutes. Let cool for several minutes before unmolding.

SPINACH QUICHES

If you have family coming, these individual quiches are the perfect option to serve to discerning palates. You can also make these crustless if time is not on your side. *Serves 6* *V*

Crust:
¾ cup whole wheat flour (preferably not pastry)

¾ cup all-purpose flour

½ teaspoon salt

⅓ cup extra-virgin olive oil

6 tablespoons cold water

Filling:
7 large eggs

¼ cup skim milk

⅓ cup crumbled soft goat cheese (about 2 ounces)

½ cup roasted red pepper, diced

1 shallot, finely chopped

1 tablespoon fresh thyme, plus more for garnish

¼ teaspoon salt

¼ teaspoon pepper

1½ cups finely chopped spinach

For the Crust: In a large bowl, stir together the whole wheat flour, all-purpose flour, and salt. Make a well in the dry ingredients and pour in the olive oil and water. Stir with a wooden spoon, form into a ball, wrap in plastic, and refrigerate for at least 30 minutes.

Preheat the oven to 400°F. Divide the dough into 6 equal balls and roll each ball into an 8-inch disc on a floured work surface. Don't worry if the discs are not completely round, as jagged edges give them a rustic appeal. Gently press each disc into a jumbo muffin cup, making sure the dough reaches the top of the sides. Stuff each cup with a wad of aluminum foil or a paper liner filled with dried beans and bake for 15 minutes. Take the muffin tin out of the oven and remove the foil or liner and beans.

For the Filling: Reduce the oven temperature to 350°F. In a large bowl, lightly beat the eggs. Stir in the milk, goat cheese, red pepper, shallot, thyme, salt, and pepper. Remove ⅔ cup of the egg mixture into a small bowl and set aside. Stir the spinach into the large bowl with the remaining egg mixture. Divide the spinach mixture among the crust-lined muffin cups. Top with the reserved egg mixture. Bake until set, about 25 minutes. Let cool for several minutes before unmolding. Garnish with fresh thyme, if desired.

QUINOA, KALE, AND FETA BAKE

This vegetarian main course rouses taste buds with a balancing act between two poles of flavor: salty and earthy. Feta cheese is salty enough, so don't add any salt. If available, try to use red quinoa for splash of color. And don't forget the olive oil for a peppery boost. Make sure to give your muffin tin a good greasing or use paper liners for these bites.   *Serves 6   G, V*

¾ cup red or white quinoa

1½ cups water

½ bunch kale, ribs removed and roughly chopped (4 to 5 cups)

1½ cups finely chopped feta cheese

3 large eggs, lightly beaten

1 large shallot, finely diced

3 garlic cloves, minced

juice of ½ lemon

1 tablespoon Sriracha hot sauce (optional)

1 tablespoon fresh thyme or 1 teaspoon dried thyme

¼ teaspoon ground nutmeg

¼ teaspoon pepper

extra-virgin olive oil, as needed

Bring the quinoa and water to a boil in a medium saucepan over high heat. Reduce the heat to low and simmer, covered, until the quinoa is tender and the water has been absorbed, about 12 minutes. Set aside to cool.

Preheat the oven to 375°F. In a food processor, pulse the kale until finely chopped. You may need to do this in two batches. Place the kale in a large bowl along with the cooked quinoa, feta cheese, eggs, shallot, garlic, lemon juice, hot sauce, if using, thyme, nutmeg, and pepper. Divide the mixture among 6 jumbo muffin cups, press down to compact, and bake until set, about 25 minutes. Let cool for several minutes before unmolding. Serve with a drizzle of olive oil over the top.

TRUSTY SIDEKICKS: SIDE DISHES

If you've always been kind of blasé about side dishes, serving the same bowl of rice or steamed broccoli, this chapter contains a riot of fun recipes sure to excite taste buds. They range from blissfully easy to sumptuously complex and help prove that the side dish need not play second fiddle to any main. And with significant levels of nutrients, they are just as good for your health as they are for your palate.

RATATOUILLE MUFFINS

The classic French side dish ratatouille is usually prepared by sautéing all the ingredients together or layering the vegetables casserole style. This version is a winner, too. Consider packing them for lunches.

Serves 6   V, G

1 tablespoon grapeseed or canola oil

1 leek, thinly sliced or 1 small onion, chopped

1½ cups diced zucchini (about 1 large)

1½ cups diced eggplant (about 1 large)

3 garlic cloves, chopped

2 teaspoons dried basil

½ teaspoon salt

¼ teaspoon red pepper flakes

½ cup chopped sun-dried tomatoes

⅓ cup sliced kalamata olives

juice of ½ lemon

3 large eggs

⅓ cup low-fat milk

¼ cup extra-virgin olive oil

1 cup whole wheat pastry flour

1 tablespoon natural cane sugar or white sugar

1 teaspoon baking powder

1 cup grated Parmesan cheese (about 4 ounces)

Preheat the oven to 350°F. Heat the oil in a large skillet over medium heat. Add the leek, zucchini, eggplant, garlic, basil, salt, and red pepper flakes, and cook until the vegetables have softened, about 5 minutes. Remove from the heat and stir in the tomatoes, olives, and lemon juice.

In a medium bowl, lightly beat the eggs. Beat in the milk and oil. In a large bowl, stir together the flour, sugar, and baking powder. Add the wet ingredients to the dry ingredients, stir to combine, then fold in the vegetables. Fold in the Parmesan cheese. Divide the mixture among 12 medium muffin cups and bake until muffins are firm to the touch, about 20 minutes. Let cool for several minutes before unmolding.

Top: RATATOUILLE MUFFINS, *page 96*
Bottom: YORKSHIRE PUDDING WITH MUSHROOM GRAVY, *page 98*

YORKSHIRE PUDDING WITH MUSHROOM GRAVY

One of my fondest memories of the holidays in the Kadey residence is my brother and me fighting over the last piece of Mom's Yorkshire pudding. This is her pudding recipe and perhaps no other is more cherished to me in this book. *Serves 6*   *V, F*

Yorkshire Pudding:
1 cup all-purpose flour
½ teaspoon salt
2 large eggs
1 cup low-fat milk
chives, for garnish

Mushroom Gravy:
1 tablespoon grapeseed or canola oil
2 shallots, chopped

10 ounces cremini mushrooms, sliced (about 4 cups)
½ cup beer, preferably wheat
3 tablespoons cornstarch
3 cups reduced-sodium vegetable broth, divided
1 tablespoon fresh thyme or 1 teaspoon dried thyme
salt and pepper

For the Yorkshire Pudding: Preheat the oven to 400°F. Generously grease 6 jumbo muffin cups with butter or shortening. Place the muffin pan in the oven for 5 minutes. Stir together the flour and salt in a large bowl. In a medium bowl, whisk together the eggs and milk. Add the wet ingredients to the dry ingredients and stir gently to combine. Divide the mixture among the hot muffin cups and bake until no longer doughy, about 28 minutes. Do not open the oven door during cooking! Let cool for a few minutes before unmolding.

For the Mushroom Gravy: While the pudding bakes, heat the oil in a medium saucepan over medium heat. Add the shallots and mushrooms, and cook until the mushrooms have softened, about 5 minutes. Add the beer, raise the heat to medium-high, and boil until the beer has reduced by half, about 3 minutes.

Meanwhile, slowly whisk the cornstarch into 1 cup of the broth until smooth and set aside. Add the remaining 2 cups broth and the thyme to the pan with the beer. Return to a boil and stir in the cornstarch mixture. Simmer until thickened, 6 to 8 minutes. Season to taste with salt and pepper. Serve the mushroom gravy with the popovers and garnish with fresh chives.

CORN CAKES

Here's a side dish that screams summer. However, when sweet corn is out of season, use frozen kernels. Feel free to toss in some shredded cheddar, Colby, or Monterey Jack.   *Serves 5*   *V, F*

1½ cups corn kernels (from about 2 ears corn)

⅓ cup whole wheat pastry flour

⅓ cup yellow cornmeal

1 jalapeño pepper, seeded and diced

1 red bell pepper, diced

1 tablespoon coconut palm sugar or other granulated sugar

juice of 1 lime

2 garlic cloves, minced

⅓ cup chopped cilantro

1 large egg, lightly beaten

¼ teaspoon salt

¼ teaspoon pepper

⅓ cup crumbled feta cheese (about 2 ounces)

Preheat the oven to 375°F. Pulse the corn several times in a food processor into coarse chunks, but do not puree. Transfer to a large bowl and stir in the whole wheat pastry flour, cornmeal, jalapeño, bell pepper, sugar, lime juice, garlic, cilantro, egg, salt, and pepper. Divide the mixture among 10 medium muffin cups and press down with the back of a spoon to flatten. Cook for 20 minutes, or until slightly golden on top and set. Let cool for several minutes before unmolding. Serve with feta cheese on top.

QUINOA-MUSHROOM CAKES WITH SRIRACHA AIOLI

These earthy cakes have a nice crunchy textural contrast from the walnuts, and Sriracha-spiked mayonnaise adds a kick.   *Serves 6*   *V, G, F*

1 cup quinoa

2 cups water

1 tablespoon grapeseed or canola oil

8 ounces button (white) or cremini mushrooms, finely chopped (about 3 cups)

1 small onion, finely diced

1 medium carrot, grated

2 large eggs

⅓ cup chopped walnuts

1 teaspoon dried thyme

¼ teaspoon salt

¼ teaspoon pepper

½ cup regular or reduced-fat mayonnaise

2 teaspoons Sriracha sauce, or to taste

1 tablespoon lemon juice

1 garlic clove, grated

Bring the quinoa and water to a boil in a medium saucepan over high heat. Reduce the heat to low and simmer, covered, until the water has been absorbed, about 15 minutes. Meanwhile, heat the oil in a medium skillet over medium heat. Add the mushrooms and onion and cook until the vegetables have softened, about 5 minutes.

Preheat the oven to 350°F. Transfer the mushroom mixture to a large bowl and stir in the cooked quinoa, carrot, eggs, walnuts, thyme, salt, and pepper. Divide the mixture among 12 medium muffin cups, making sure to pack down the contents. Bake until set and golden on top, about 30 minutes. Let cool for several minutes before unmolding.

To make the aioli, stir together the mayonnaise, Sriracha sauce, lemon juice, and garlic in a small bowl and mix well. Serve over the quinoa cakes.

BROCCOLI-BEAN CAKES WITH GARLIC-LEMON BUTTER SAUCE

Here's a good way to get the little ones (and the grown-up ones) to eat their broccoli and beans.   *Serves 6   V, F*

Cakes:

1 head of broccoli, cut into florets (about 5 cups)

1 (15-ounce) can white navy beans, drained and rinsed

2 large eggs

¾ cup panko (Japanese-style) bread crumbs, divided

1 shallot, finely chopped

3 tablespoons hemp seeds (optional)

1 tablespoon red wine vinegar

½ teaspoon salt

¼ teaspoon pepper

Butter Sauce:

¼ cup (½ stick) unsalted butter, chopped

3 to 4 garlic cloves, finely minced

juice of ½ lemon

pinch of salt

For the Cakes: Preheat the oven to 375°F. Place the broccoli florets in a food processor and process until the broccoli has been pulverized into small bits. If you don't have a food processor, simply chop very finely with a knife. Add the broccoli to a large bowl with the navy beans and mash gently. Stir in the eggs, ½ cup of the panko bread crumbs, and the shallot, hemp seeds, if using, red wine vinegar, salt, and pepper. Divide the mixture among 12 medium muffin cups, making sure to pack the contents tightly. Sprinkle the tops with the remaining panko bread crumbs and press down gently. Bake for 20 minutes, then turn on the oven's broiler and heat until the bread crumbs on top are toasted, about 1 minute more. Let cool for several minutes before unmolding.

    For the Butter Sauce: Place the butter and garlic in a small saucepan over low heat. Once the butter has melted, stir in the lemon juice and salt, and heat for 2 minutes. Serve over the broccoli bean cakes.

SAMOSA PUFFS WITH GREEN CHUTNEY

Indian-inspired dishes are notorious for giving your spice rack a good workout. These no-fry, open-faced samosas are no exception.
Serves 6   V

Samosas:

1 tablespoon grapeseed or canola oil

1 medium russet or Yukon Gold potato, finely diced

1 small onion, finely diced

1 tablespoon minced fresh ginger

½ teaspoon ground cumin

½ teaspoon fennel seeds (optional)

½ teaspoon ground coriander

¼ teaspoon ground turmeric

⅛ teaspoon cayenne pepper

¼ teaspoon salt

¼ teaspoon black pepper

½ cup frozen peas

¼ cup chopped unsalted raw cashews

1 teaspoon garam masala

juice of ½ lemon

7 ounces puff pastry (½ package), thawed

Chutney:

2 cups tightly packed fresh cilantro

½ cup tightly packed fresh mint

¼ cup unsweetened dried shredded coconut

¼ cup extra-virgin olive oil

juice of ½ lemon

1 tablespoon grated fresh ginger

2 garlic cloves, grated

1 serrano or jalapeño pepper, seeded and diced

½ teaspoon ground cumin

¼ teaspoon salt

For the Samosas: Heat the oil in a large skillet over medium heat. Add the potato and cook for 10 minutes. Stir in the onion and cook until the potato is tender and onion has softened, about 6 minutes more. Stir in the ginger, cumin, fennel, if using, coriander, turmeric, cayenne pepper, salt, and black pepper, and cook 1 minute. Add the peas and cashews and cook for 2 minutes. Remove from the heat and stir in the garam masala and lemon juice. Let cool.

Preheat the oven to 400°F. On a lightly floured work surface, roll out the puff pastry into a 12-inch square. Using a knife or pizza wheel, cut the pastry into 12 rectangular pieces by slicing 4 vertical rows and 3 horizontal rows. Stuff the rectangles into 12 medium muffin cups and poke the bottoms with a fork to prevent puffing. Divide the potato mixture among the pastry cups and bake until the pastry is crispy and golden, about 15 minutes. Let cool for a few minutes before unmolding.

For the Chutney: Place all of the chutney ingredients in a food processor and process until well combined and the herbs have been reduced to small bits. Serve with the samosa puffs.

BUTTERNUT SQUASH SOUFFLÉS

Here's proof that a soufflé doesn't need to be a monumental kitchen task or torpedo your diet.   *Serves 6*   V

½ pound butternut squash, peeled and diced (about 2 cups)

3 tablespoons flour, divided

2 tablespoons unsalted butter

1 small onion, finely chopped

1 tablespoon chopped fresh sage or 1 teaspoon dried sage

¼ teaspoon pepper

½ cup low-fat milk

6 canned anchovy fillets, or to taste, finely chopped (optional)

½ cup shredded Gruyère cheese (about 2 ounces), plus more to serve

3 large eggs, separated

Steam or boil the butternut squash until very tender. Transfer to a medium bowl and mash with a fork or potato masher. You only need 1 cup butternut puree for this recipe, so reserve any extra for another use. Let cool to room temperature.

Preheat the oven to 375°F. Generously grease 12 medium muffin cups with butter and dust with 1 tablespoon of the flour. Tap out any excess flour. In a medium saucepan, melt the butter over medium-low heat. Add the onion, sage, and pepper. Cook, stirring often, until the onion is softened, 6 to 8 minutes. Stir in the remaining 2 tablespoons flour and cook for 3 minutes, stirring often. Gradually add the milk, whisking constantly until thickened, about 2 minutes. Remove from heat and stir in the mashed squash, anchovies, if using, and Gruyère cheese. Whisk in the egg yolks one at a time.

In a clean medium bowl, beat the egg whites with a whisk or electric mixer on medium speed until stiff peaks form. Whisk one-quarter of the egg whites into the squash mixture, then gently fold in the rest. Divide the mixture among the prepared muffin cups and bake until puffed and golden brown on top, about 18 minutes. Resist the temptation to open the oven door during cooking, as this can muck up the rising. Let cool for several minutes before unmolding. The soufflés will take a nose dive in the middle upon cooling. Serve with additional shredded cheese on top.

Top: BUTTERNUT SQUASH SOUFFLÉS, *page 104*
Bottom: SWEET POTATO—SWISS CHARD GRATINS, *page 106*

SWEET POTATO—SWISS CHARD GRATINS

Who says a gratin has to arrive at the dinner table in a casserole dish? These three-tier taste bombs won't disappoint. Make sure to purchase sweet potatoes that are not too wide so that the sliced rounds will fit into medium-size muffin cups. Roasting the potato slices instead of boiling, steaming, or microwaving them adds an extra flavor dimension.   *Serves 6   V, G, F*

1½ pounds sweet potato (about 3 medium)

2 teaspoons grapeseed or canola oil

¼ teaspoon salt

¼ teaspoon pepper

1½ cups shredded regular or reduced-fat white cheddar cheese (about 6 ounces), divided

1 cup reduced-fat sour cream

1 tablespoon chopped fresh rosemary or thyme

½ teaspoon paprika, sweet or smoked

¼ teaspoon ground nutmeg

1 cup chopped Swiss chard

Preheat the oven to 400°F. Slice the sweet potato into 36 rounds ¼ inch thick and toss with the oil, salt, and pepper. Spread out the rounds on a baking sheet and bake until tender, about 20 minutes.

Meanwhile, in a medium bowl, stir together 1 cup of the cheddar cheese and the sour cream, rosemary, paprika, and nutmeg. Place a roasted sweet potato round in each of 12 medium muffin cups. Divide one-half of the cheese mixture and one-half of the Swiss chard among the muffin cups. Place a second sweet potato round on top of the greens, and top with the remaining cheese mixture and Swiss chard. Place a third sweet potato round over the chard and sprinkle with the remaining ½ cup cheddar cheese. Bake until the cheese is melted and bubbly, about 10 minutes. Let cool for several minutes before unmolding.

ROASTED GARLIC CORNBREAD

Pumped full of garlic loveliness, these individual cornbreads are best made jumbo-size so it takes longer before only crumbs are left on my plate. You certainly can prepare them in medium muffin cups, but you'll need to reduce cooking time by a few minutes. Serve warm with butter.

Serves 6   V, F

2 small garlic bulbs

1¼ cup coarsely ground yellow cornmeal

¾ cup whole wheat pastry flour

2 tablespoons coconut palm sugar or other granulated sugar

¾ teaspoon salt

2 teaspoons baking powder

½ teaspoon baking soda

1 tablespoon fresh thyme or 1 teaspoon dried thyme

2 large eggs

1 cup buttermilk

¼ cup extra-virgin olive oil

¾ cup grated Parmesan cheese (about 3 ounces)

Preheat the oven to 375°F. Grease 6 jumbo muffin cups with butter. Remove any excess papery covering on the garlic bulbs and slice off the tops of the bulbs so most of the cloves are exposed. Wrap the bulbs in foil and bake until the garlic is very soft, about 40 minutes. Remove from the oven and increase the temperature to 400°F. Once cool enough to handle, use a fork to scrape out the garlic pulp into a small bowl and mash well.

In a large bowl, whisk together the cornmeal, whole wheat pastry flour, sugar, salt, baking powder, baking soda, and thyme. In a second large bowl, lightly beat the eggs and whisk in the buttermilk and olive oil. Stir in the mashed garlic. Add the dry ingredients to the wet ingredients, stir to combine, then fold in the Parmesan cheese.

Divide the batter among the prepared muffin cups and bake until golden and an inserted toothpick comes out clean, about 15 minutes. Let cool 5 minutes before unmolding.

EDAMAME-STUFFED RUTABAGA CUPS

Although commonly compared to turnips, the larger rutabaga has a sweeter flavor with less of a peppery bite. When cooked and mashed, it is a wonderful alternative to potatoes in recipes. *Serves 6*   *V, F*

3 pounds rutabaga, peeled and chopped

½ cup whole wheat pastry flour or other flour

2 tablespoons unsalted butter

1 tablespoon fresh thyme

2 teaspoons grainy or Dijon mustard

½ teaspoon salt

¼ teaspoon black pepper

¼ teaspoon ground nutmeg

1 cup frozen shelled edamame

juice of ½ lemon

¼ teaspoon cayenne pepper

salt

Steam or boil the rutabaga until very tender. Transfer the cooked rutabaga to a bowl of a food processor along with the flour, butter, thyme, mustard, salt, black pepper, and nutmeg. Blend until well combined. You can also do this in a large bowl using a potato masher or even a fork.

Preheat the oven to 375°F. Bring a medium pot of water to a boil over high heat. Add the edamame and cook until tender, about 5 minutes. Place the edamame, lemon juice, cayenne pepper, and salt to taste in a food processor and process until the edamane has been reduced to tiny bits. Fill 12 medium muffin cups halfway with the rutabaga mixture. Make a small indentation in each with your finger and evenly distribute the edamame mixture among the cups. Top with the remaining rutabaga mixture. You may have some rutabaga left over. Bake until nicely browned on top, about 30 minutes. Let cool for several minutes before unmolding. To unmold, run a butter knife around the edges, place a flat object such as a cutting board over the muffin tin, and turn the muffin tin upside down.

Top: EDAMAME-STUFFED RUTABAGA CUPS, *page 108*
Bottom: RICE-VEGGIE BAKE WITH ALMOND CREAM SAUCE, *page 110*

RICE-VEGGIE BAKE WITH ALMOND CREAM SAUCE

Here's a nice package of whole grains and vegetables that also works well for weekday lunches. *Serves 4* V, G, F

Rice-Veggie Bake:
½ cup Wehani rice or other brown rice

1 cup water

1 tablespoon grapeseed or canola oil

1 shallot, finely diced

1 small red bell pepper, finely chopped

½ cup fresh or frozen green peas

1 teaspoon dried thyme

½ teaspoon salt

½ teaspoon ground coriander

4 large eggs

¼ cup unflavored almond milk or other milk

Sauce:
2 cups unflavored almond milk

½ cup low-sodium vegetable broth

⅓ cup whole almonds

2 green onions, white and green parts, thinly sliced

2 small crushed dried red chiles or ⅛ teaspoon cayenne pepper

juice of ½ lemon

For the Rice-Veggie Bake: Bring the rice and water to a boil over high heat. Reduce the heat to low and simmer, covered, until tender and the water has been absorbed, about 30 minutes.

Preheat oven to 375°F. In a medium skillet, heat the oil over medium heat. Add the shallot, bell pepper, and peas, and cook until the vegetables are tender, about 4 minutes. Stir in the thyme, salt, and coriander, and cook 1 minute more. In a large bowl, lightly beat the eggs with the almond milk. Stir in the rice and the vegetable mixture. Divide the mixture among 10 medium muffin cups and bake until set, about 18 minutes.

For the Sauce: Combine all the sauce ingredients in a medium saucepan over medium heat. Bring to a simmer and cook until reduced by half, about 20 minutes. Carefully puree in a blender and serve over the rice cakes.

MASHED POTATO CUPS WITH CURRY SOUR CREAM

Kids and adults alike eat up this riff on an iconic side dish. If desired, gussy these up by adding diced ham or bacon. If avoiding gluten, use a gluten-free flour blend. You can omit the curry powder if you prefer to serve these with plain sour cream.   *Serves 6   V*

2 pounds Yukon Gold potatoes, peeled and diced

2 tablespoons unsalted butter

⅓ cup buttermilk or low-fat milk

¼ cup whole wheat pastry flour

2 tablespoons chopped fresh sage

1 tablespoon grainy or Dijon mustard

2 large eggs, lightly beaten

¼ teaspoon ground nutmeg

¼ teaspoon salt

¼ teaspoon pepper

½ cup low-fat sour cream

½ teaspoon curry powder

Steam or boil the potatoes until very tender. Preheat the oven to 375°F. Transfer the potatoes to a large bowl and mash with the butter, buttermilk or milk, flour, sage, mustard, eggs, nutmeg, salt, and pepper. Make sure to leave the mixture slightly chunky. Divide the potato mixture among 12 medium muffin cups. Bake until set, about 25 minutes. Let cool for several minutes before unmolding. In a small bowl, stir together the sour cream and curry powder. Serve the mashed potato cups with the curry cream.

SAVORY SMOKED SALMON AND CHEESE MUFFINS

These savory muffins are ideal for a quick lunch fix. Similar to the other savory muffins in this chapter, these are best served warm. Try to use wild smoked salmon, which is a more sustainable option than farmed.

Serves 12

1½ cups whole wheat pastry flour or spelt flour

½ cup finely ground yellow cornmeal

1½ teaspoons baking powder

2 tablespoons finely chopped chives

2 tablespoons coconut palm sugar or other granulated sugar

½ teaspoon smoked paprika (optional)

½ teaspoon garlic powder

½ teaspoon salt

2 large eggs

½ cup low-fat milk

½ cup low-fat sour cream

¼ cup melted coconut oil or other oil

1 red bell pepper, finely diced

1 cup shredded cheddar cheese, preferably sharp

2 ounces smoked wild salmon, chopped

Preheat the oven to 375°F. In a large bowl, stir together the flour, cornmeal, baking powder, chives, sugar, smoked paprika, if using, garlic powder, and salt. In a separate bowl, lightly beat the eggs and whisk in the milk, sour cream, and oil. Add the wet ingredients to the dry ingredients and stir gently to combine. Fold in the bell pepper, cheese, and smoked salmon. Divide the mixture among 12 medium muffin cups and bake until golden on top and an inserted toothpick comes out clean, about 20 minutes. Let cool several minutes before unmolding.

JALAPEÑO CHEESE ROLLS

These slightly spicy cheesy pizza rolls are a great option when you need lunch in a hurry. You can use store-bought pizza dough or make your own using my no-fail recipe (see page 71). *Serves 4*   *V, F*

10 ounces whole wheat pizza dough

1 (8-ounce) skinless, boneless chicken breast, cooked and finely diced or shredded

½ cup finely chopped roasted red pepper

1 medium jalapeño pepper, seeded and finely diced

1 teaspoon dried oregano

½ cup shredded cheddar cheese (about 2 ounces)

½ cup shredded mozzarella cheese (about 2 ounces)

¼ teaspoon salt

Preheat the oven to 400°F. On a floured work surface, roll the pizza dough into a rectangle about 12 x 8 inches. Spread the chicken, red pepper, jalapeño, oregano, cheddar cheese, mozzarella cheese, and salt on top. Resist the urge to add too much topping, which can make rolling the dough difficult. Tightly roll up the dough and pinch the ends to seal. Slice into 8 equal pieces and roll each piece into a ball. Drop the balls into 8 medium muffin cups and bake until golden, 18 to 20 minutes. Let cool for several minutes before unmolding.

SPINACH DINNER ROLLS

This recipe requires some extra kitchen time, but one bite into these amped-up rolls and you'll be glad you put in the effort. To save time, frozen spinach can be used. Just make sure to squeeze out the excess liquid.　*Serves 6*　*V, F*

¾ cup milk

1 packet (2¼ teaspoons) active dry yeast

1 large egg

2 tablespoons extra-virgin olive oil

1 tablespoon sugar

1 tablespoon fresh thyme or 1 teaspoon dried thyme

½ teaspoon salt

1½ cups all-purpose flour or bread flour

1 cup whole wheat pastry flour

1 pound spinach (about 2 bunches), stems sliced off

1 cup finely diced feta cheese

In a small saucepan, warm the milk until just before it simmers. Transfer to a large bowl, stir in the yeast and let stand until the yeast has dissolved, about 5 minutes. Whisk in the egg, olive oil, sugar, thyme, and salt. Stir in the all-purpose or bread flour and the whole wheat pastry flour until the mixture clumps together.

Place the dough on a floured work surface and knead until the dough is smooth and elastic, about 5 minutes. If an indentation remains in the dough when pressed with your finger, it's ready for rising. Place the dough in a large bowl with a little oil, turn to coat, and cover with a clean kitchen towel. Set aside in a warm, draft-free place until roughly doubled in size, about 1 hour.

Meanwhile, blanch the spinach by bringing a large pot of water to a boil and filling a large bowl with ice water. Add the spinach to the pot and boil until bright green in color, about 30 seconds. Drain and transfer to the ice water for about 2 minutes. Drain and squeeze out as much water as possible between several sheets of paper towel or a clean kitchen towel. Chop the spinach.

Punch down the dough by pushing down in the center of the dough with your fist and then pushing the edges into the center using your fingertips. Transfer to a floured work surface and press into a square. Roll the dough into a roughly 20 x 10-inch rectangle, with the long end at the bottom of the work surface. Spread the spinach on top of the dough, leaving a 1-inch border around the edges. Sprinkle the feta cheese on top of the spinach and tightly roll the dough into a long cylinder. Pinch the ends together to seal, and slice the cylinder into 12 equal pieces. Divide the dough pieces among 12 medium muffin cups with one of the spinach sides facing down. Cover with a clean kitchen towel and let rise for 1 hour in a warm, draft-free place.

Preheat the oven to 375°F. Bake the rolls until the tops are golden, about 18 minutes. Let cool before unmolding. Serve warm.

CHEDDAR-SAGE BISCUITS

These are not as dense as your typical biscuit, but all the wonderful savory flavors are still there. The biscuits are best consumed within a day of baking, or you can freeze them in an airtight container for several weeks.   *Serves 5   V, F*

1¼ cups whole wheat flour (preferably not pastry)

1 cup all-purpose flour or bread flour

1 tablespoon coconut palm sugar or other granulated sugar

2 teaspoons baking powder

¾ teaspoon baking soda

½ teaspoon salt

1 teaspoon garlic powder

¼ cup (½ stick) cold unsalted butter, cut into ½-inch cubes

1½ cups shredded sharp cheddar cheese (about 6 ounces)

¼ cup finely chopped fresh sage or 2 teaspoons dried sage

1 cup buttermilk

Preheat the oven to 400°F. In a food processor, pulse together the whole wheat flour, all-purpose or bread flour, sugar, baking powder, baking soda, salt, and garlic powder. Pulse in the butter until mixture looks like coarse meal and the butter is no larger than small pebbles. You can also do this in a bowl with a pastry cutter. Transfer the mixture to a bowl and fold in the cheddar cheese and sage. Add the buttermilk and combine gently until a dough forms.

Divide the mixture among 10 medium muffin cups and bake until golden on top, about 15 minutes. Let cool several minutes before unmolding. Serve warm with honey or butter.

Top: CHEDDAR-SAGE BISCUITS, *page 116*

Bottom: TOMATO-EGG TARTLETTES, *page 118*

TOMATO-EGG TARTLETTES

These downsized treats prove tarts don't have to be a dietary train wreck. If you want to keep the crust crispy when serving leftovers, use the oven rather than the microwave to reheat.   *Serves 6*   V

Crust:

¾ cup whole wheat flour (preferably not pastry)

¾ cup all-purpose flour or bread flour

½ teaspoon salt

1 tablespoon chopped fresh rosemary or 1 teaspoon dried rosemary

⅓ cup extra-virgin olive oil

6 tablespoons cold water

Filling:

3 large eggs

⅓ cup low-fat milk

1 cup shredded Gruyère cheese or other Swiss-style cheese (about 4 ounces), divided

2 tablespoons chopped fresh basil

2 teaspoons grainy or Dijon mustard

½ teaspoon smoked paprika (optional)

¼ teaspoon salt

¼ teaspoon pepper

2 plum (Roma) tomatoes

For the Crust: In a large bowl, combine the whole wheat flour, all-purpose or bread flour, salt, and rosemary. Make a well in the dry ingredients and pour in the olive oil and water. Mix to form a dough, wrap in plastic, and refrigerate for at least 30 minutes.

Preheat the oven to 400°F. Dived the dough into 12 small balls and roll each ball into about a 6-inch disc on a floured work surface. Gently press the discs into medium muffin cups, making sure the dough rises up to the top of the sides. Stuff each cup with a wad of aluminum foil or a paper liner filled with dried beans and bake for 15 minutes.

For the Filling: Meanwhile, in a large bowl, lightly beat the eggs and milk. Stir in ½ cup of the cheese and the basil, mustard, paprika, salt, and pepper. Slice the tomatoes into thin rounds and cut each round in half to form half moons.

Remove the aluminum foil or liner and beans from the crust cups and fill the bottoms with the remaining ½ cup cheese. Top with the egg mixture and place two tomato half moons in each cup over the egg mixture. Bake until the eggs are set, about 15 minutes. Let cool for a few minutes before unmolding, and garnish with fresh pepper.

STUFFINS

Here's a way to make your kitchen redolent of Thanksgiving any time of year. The best way to serve these is warm and doused with Mushroom Gravy (see page 98). *Serves 6   V, F*

1 day-old whole wheat baguette

1 tablespoon grapeseed or canola oil

1 leek, thinly sliced and then chopped

2 celery ribs, thinly sliced

1 teaspoon dried sage

1 teaspoon dried thyme

¼ teaspoon salt

¼ teaspoon pepper

1 cup grated Parmesan cheese

½ cup dried cranberries

1 medium apple, finely diced

2 large eggs

⅓ cup low-fat milk

⅔ cup reduced-sodium vegetable or chicken broth, or as needed

Preheat the oven to 375°F. Slice the bread into small cubes and place in a very large bowl. You want about 4 cups total. Heat the oil in a skillet over medium heat. Add the leek, celery, sage, thyme, salt, and pepper. Cook until the leek and celery are tender, about 5 minutes. Add the cooked vegetables to the bowl with the bread cubes along with the Parmesan cheese, cranberries, and apple, and stir to combine.

In a small bowl, whisk together the eggs and milk. Pour over the bread mixture and stir to combine. Pour in ⅓ cup of the broth and stir to combine. Add the remaining ⅓ cup broth and stir until everything is moist. Add more broth as needed. Divide the bread mixture among 12 medium muffin cups. Use the back of a fork to pack the muffin cups tightly with the bread mixture. Bake until the tops are nicely browned, about 30 minutes. Let cool for several minutes before unmolding.

BLACK BEAN CUPS WITH SMOKY AVOCADO

The earthy flavor of black beans and bright avocado team up to produce an exciting side dish. Available at most grocers, smoked paprika should be in every pantry.   *Serves 6   V, G*

Bean Cups:
1 (15-ounce) can black beans, drained and rinsed
½ cup quinoa flour
⅓ cup chopped parsley
1 teaspoon ground cumin
½ teaspoon salt
¼ teaspoon pepper
2 tablespoons extra-virgin olive oil

Avocado Filling:
1 ripe avocado
1 plum (Roma) tomato, seeded and diced
½ teaspoon smoked paprika
½ teaspoon grated lime zest
juice of ½ lime
1 garlic clove, grated or finely minced
salt

For the Bean Cups: Preheat the oven to 350°F. Place the black beans, quinoa flour, parsley, cumin, salt, pepper, and olive oil in a food processor and process until a paste forms. Place a heaping spoonful of the bean mixture into 10 medium muffin cups and form each into a cup with the paste coming up the sides. Bake until the cups have set but are still slightly moist, about 20 minutes. Let cool for several minutes before unmolding.

   For the Avocado Filling: Place the avocado in a medium bowl and mash. Stir in the tomato, paprika, lime zest, lime juice, garlic, and salt to taste. Add a generous dollop to each black bean cup.

SAVE ROOM FOR... DESSERT

If the only sweet treat you use your muffin tin for is the eponymous baked good, boy are you missing out. From panna cottas to mini tarts to individual cheesecakes, a muffin tray can turn out no shortage of virtuous desserts. I am particularly bullish on taking cake recipes and dividing them up into muffin cups. Not only does it slash baking time, but it also helps ensure portion control.

If you have an aversion to the D word, fearing an iffy ingredient list that contains a hazardous trifecta of white flour, copious amounts of heavily refined sugar, and a heart-stopping amount of fat, fear not. The arsenal of dessert recipes that follow are chock-full of wholesome ingredients such as whole grain flours, nuts, and naturally sweet fruits with just the right amount of sweeteners so they won't send your blood sugar into a tizzy. You'll find recipes from the deliciously simple (no-bake cheesecake, yum!) to splendidly complex— I'm looking at you, Mr. Apple Pie—that up the ante on a great meal.

EXTRA-MOIST CHOCOLATE CAKES

These almost-flourless cakes are the epitome of chocolate indulgence, with a short baking time that assures a warm, ooey-gooey dark chocolate center. *Serves 6 V*

4 ounces dark chocolate, chopped

¼ cup (½ stick) unsalted butter, diced

1 large whole egg

1 large egg yolk

⅓ cup coconut palm sugar or other granulated sugar

2 tablespoons whole wheat pastry flour

1 teaspoon vanilla extract

½ teaspoon ground cinnamon

⅛ teaspoon salt

⅛ teaspoon cayenne pepper or chili powder (optional)

2 teaspoons instant espresso powder or very finely ground coffee dissolved in 2 tablespoons boiling water (optional)

confectioners' sugar, for dusting (optional)

raspberries, for garnish (optional)

Grease 6 medium muffin cups with butter. Melt the chocolate and butter in a double boiler or a heatproof bowl set over a pan of lightly simmering water, stirring often. Or, microwave the chocolate and butter in a large microwave-safe bowl in 25-second increments on high power, stirring after each interval until melted.

In a medium bowl using an electric mixer on medium speed or a metal whisk, whisk together the whole egg, egg yolk, and sugar until thickened and paler in color. Fold the egg mixture into the chocolate mixture. Stir in the flour, vanilla extract, cinnamon, salt, and cayenne pepper or chili powder, if using, and mix well. If using the espresso powder dissolved in boiling water, stir it into the batter. Divide the mixture among the prepared muffin cups and refrigerate for 30 minutes.

Preheat the oven to 375°F. Remove the muffin tin from the refrigerator and bake until the tops are just barely set, about 8 minutes. Let cool for several minutes before unmolding. To unmold, run a butter knife around the edges and invert onto serving plates. Dust with confectioners' sugar and garnish with raspberries, if desired.

Top: EXTRA-MOIST CHOCOLATE CAKES, *page 122*
Bottom: CARROT CAKES WITH MAPLE FROSTING, *page 124*

CARROT CAKES WITH MAPLE FROSTING AND CANDIED CARROT

By cutting down on the sweetness and using whole grain flours, these are more carrot cake than cupcake.   *Serves 10   V, F*

Carrot Cakes:
1¼ cups whole wheat pastry flour
½ cup quinoa flour
1 teaspoon baking powder
¾ teaspoon baking soda
1 teaspoon ground ginger
½ teaspoon ground cinnamon
½ teaspoon ground cloves
½ teaspoon salt
2 large eggs
⅔ cup coconut palm sugar or other granulated sugar
1 teaspoon vanilla extract

⅓ cup melted coconut oil or other oil
1½ cups shredded carrot
1 cup crushed canned pineapple, drained

Frosting:
5 tablespoons cream cheese, at room temperature
2 tablespoons pure maple syrup
½ teaspoon vanilla extract

Candied Carrots:
2 medium carrots, peeled
⅓ cup coconut palm sugar or other granulated sugar
3 tablespoons water

For the Carrot Cakes: Preheat the oven to 350°F. In a large bowl, stir together the whole wheat pastry flour, quinoa flour, baking powder, baking soda, ginger, cinnamon, cloves, and salt. In a second large bowl, lightly beat the eggs and stir in the sugar, vanilla extract, oil, carrot, and pineapple. Add the wet ingredients to the dry ingredients and stir gently to combine. Divide the mixture among 10 medium muffin cups and bake for 20 minutes, or until an inserted toothpick comes out clean. Let cool for several minutes before unmolding.

For the Frosting: While the cakes bake, in a small bowl, whip together cream cheese, maple syrup, and vanilla extract with a fork. Spread over the cooled carrot cakes.

For the Candied Carrots: Use a vegetable peeler to create long strips of carrot. In a small saucepan over high heat, bring the sugar and water to a boil. Add the carrot strips, reduce the heat to low, and gently simmer for 10 minutes. Remove from the heat and let sit for about 5 minutes. Remove the carrot, let cool on a wire rack, then chop finely. Place about 1 teaspoon of candied carrot on each cake.

LEMON CAKES WITH BLUEBERRY COMPOTE

These lovely light and tangy lemon cakes will brighten up even the lousiest of days.   *Serves 12   V, F*

Cakes:

1¾ cups white pastry flour

2 teaspoons baking powder

¼ teaspoon salt

3 large eggs, at room temperature

⅔ cup natural cane sugar or other light-colored granulated sugar

1 cup low-fat plain yogurt

⅓ cup grapeseed or canola oil

grated zest of 1 lemon

juice of 1 lemon

Glaze:

2 tablespoons lemon juice

2 tablespoons light-colored granulated sugar

Blueberry Compote:

2 cups fresh or frozen blueberries

⅓ cup plus 1 tablespoon water, divided

¼ cup pure maple syrup

1 teaspoon ground cinnamon

½ teaspoon almond extract

2 teaspoons cornstarch

For the Cakes: Preheat the oven to 350°F. In a large bowl, sift together the flour, baking powder, and salt. In a medium bowl, beat the eggs and sugar with a whisk or electric mixer on medium speed until light and frothy. Beat in the yogurt, oil, lemon zest, and lemon juice. Add the wet ingredients to the dry ingredients and stir gently to combine. Divide the mixture among 12 medium muffin cups and bake until an inserted toothpick comes out clean, about 20 minutes.

For the Glaze: In a small bowl, whisk together the lemon juice and sugar until smooth. While the hot cakes are still in the pan, poke each cake several times with a toothpick and brush the tops with glaze. Let the glaze soak in and repeat. Unmold the cakes and cool on a wire rack.

For the Blueberry Compote: Place the blueberries, ⅓ cup of the water, and the maple syrup, cinnamon, and almond extract in a medium saucepan. Bring to a boil over high heat, reduce the heat to medium-low, and simmer, stirring occasionally, or until the blueberries have softened and begun to break down, about 20 minutes. Dissolve the cornstarch in the remaining 1 tablespoon water. Stir into the blueberry mixture and heat until thickened, about 1 minute. Serve the blueberry compote with the lemon cakes.

SWEET POTATO BROWNIE BITES

Pureed sweet potato provides these party-size brownies with moisture, earthy sweetness, and a fudgelike consistency. Not to mention it makes them a little more guilt-free if you happen to sneak a few extra. Warning—they're habit forming!   *Serves 12   V, F*

½ pound sweet potato, peeled and diced (about 1 medium)

¼ cup (½ stick) unsalted butter

1 large egg

⅔ cup unsweetened cocoa powder

⅔ cup coconut palm sugar or other granulated sugar

1 teaspoon vanilla extract

2 teaspoons grated fresh ginger or 1 teaspoon ground ginger (optional)

½ cup whole wheat pastry flour

1 teaspoon ground cinnamon

¼ teaspoon baking powder

¼ teaspoon salt

⅛ teaspoon cayenne pepper (optional)

⅓ cup cream cheese, at room temperature

2 tablespoons pure maple syrup

2 tablespoons cocoa nibs

Steam, boil, or roast the sweet potato until very tender, transfer to a large bowl, and mash with the butter.

Preheat the oven to 350°F. Add the egg, cocoa powder, sugar, vanilla extract, and ginger, if using, to the potato mixture and stir with a wooden spoon. In a second large bowl, stir together the flour, cinnamon, baking powder, salt, and cayenne pepper, if using. Stir the sugar and potato mixture into the dry ingredients and mix until no dry parts are visible. Divide the mixture among 24 mini muffin cups. Bake until an inserted toothpick comes out nearly clean, about 15 minutes. Let cool for several minutes before unmolding.

To make the frosting, beat together the cream cheese and maple syrup with a whisk or electric mixer on medium speed until smooth. Spread on top of the brownies and sprinkle with cocoa nibs.

Top: SWEET POTATO BROWNIE BITES, *page 126*
Bottom: NO-BAKE CHEESECAKES WITH RASPBERRY SAUCE, *page 128*

NO-BAKE CHEESECAKES WITH RASPBERRY SAUCE

Here's proof that you don't need to fire up the oven to luxuriate in an ambrosial dessert.   *Serves 12   V*

Cheesecakes:

1 cup graham cracker crumbs

⅔ cup finely chopped walnuts

⅓ cup pure maple syrup

1 teaspoon ground ginger (optional)

6 ounces regular or reduced-fat cream cheese, at room temperature

⅔ cup reduced-fat ricotta cheese

juice of ½ lemon

2 tablespoons natural cane sure or other light-colored granulated sugar

1 teaspoon vanilla extract

Raspberry Sauce:

2 cups raspberries

¼ cup water

2 tablespoons coconut palm sugar or other granulated sugar

juice of ½ lemon

2 teaspoons cornstarch

1 tablespoon water

For the Cheesecakes: Line 12 medium muffin cups with paper liners. In a large bowl, stir together the graham cracker crumbs, walnuts, maple syrup, and ginger, if using, until everything is moist. Add a small amount of additional maple syrup, if needed. In a second large bowl, use a fork to stir together the cream cheese, ricotta cheese, lemon juice, sugar, and vanilla extract until smooth. Divide the crumb mixture among the prepared muffin cups and press down flat. Divide the cheese mixture among the muffin cups and use a butter knife to smooth the tops. Place the muffin tin in the refrigerator to chill overnight.

For the Raspberry Sauce: Combine the raspberries, water, sugar, and lemon juice in a small saucepan over medium-low heat. Simmer until the raspberries have broken down, about 10 minutes. In a small bowl, dissolve the cornstarch in the water. Add to the sauce and heat for 1 minute. Let cool before serving over the cheesecakes.

PETITE PIES

The allure of fruit pies is unmistakable. I've provided two fruit fillings that are sure to please, but certainly other classics like strawberry-rhubarb, cherry, plum, or blueberry will do wonderfully. *Serves 12* V

1½ cups all-purpose flour

1 cup whole wheat pastry flour

1 tablespoon coconut palm sugar or other granulated sugar

1 teaspoon salt

1 cup (2 sticks) cold unsalted butter, cut into ½-inch cubes

½ cup ice water

2 tablespoons apple cider vinegar

1 large egg mixed with 1 tablespoon water, for egg wash

pie filling (see pages 130–31)

coarse sugar, for sprinkling (optional)

In a food processor, pulse together the all-purpose flour, whole wheat pastry flour, sugar, and salt. Add the cubes of cold butter and process in short pulses until you get a mixture that resembles pea-sized chunks. Or, use a pastry cutter to rub the butter into the mixture until crumbly. In a small bowl, stir together the ice water and the cider vinegar. If using a food processor, transfer the flour mixture to a large bowl. Slowly drizzle in the vinegar mixture. Combine with a spatula or wooden spoon until you can pinch the dough and it holds together. If the mixture is too dry, add more water 1 tablespoon at a time, being very careful not to make it too moist. Place the dough on a lightly floured surface, cut in half, and flatten into two discs. Wrap the discs individually in plastic wrap or wax paper and refrigerate for at least 1 hour.

Preheat the oven to 425°F. Lightly butter 12 medium muffin cups. Divide one disc of dough into 12 equal pieces. On a floured work surface, roll out each piece into a ⅛-inch-thick disc, making sure the discs are big enough to fill the muffin cups with some overhang. Press 6 discs into the muffin cups and fill each with half of your desired pie filling. Place the remaining 6 circles over each pie cup and crimp the dough together around the edges to seal. Repeat with second disc of dough and remaining pie filling.

Using a small paring knife, cut four small slits in the tops of each pie to allow for venting. Using a pastry brush, brush the tops with egg wash and sprinkle with coarse sugar, if desired. Bake for 15 minutes, then reduce the oven temperature to 350°F and bake until the crust is golden brown, about 15 minutes longer. Let cool for several minutes before unmolding, then transfer to a metal rack to cool further.

PEACH PIE FILLING

Makes enough for 12 petite pies

2 pounds peaches (about 6 medium)

2 tablespoons flour

1 tablespoon cornstarch

¼ cup coconut palm sugar or other granulated sugar

1 tablespoon lemon juice

1 teaspoon ground cinnamon

1 teaspoon grated fresh ginger (optional)

1 teaspoon vanilla extract

Bring a large pot of water to a boil. Slice an X in the bottom of each peach. Place the peaches in the boiling water for about 20 seconds and remove with a slotted spoon. Slide the peels off. Dice the peaches and mix with the remaining ingredients in a large bowl. If the mixture is very liquidy, drain off some of the excess (peaches vary in their degree of juiciness). Fill the pie crusts with the peach filling and bake as instructed.

APPLE PIE FILLING

Makes enough for 12 petite pies

1½ pounds apples (about 6 medium), such as Empire or Idared, peeled and cut into ½-inch cubes

3 tablespoons pure maple syrup

2 tablespoons whole wheat pastry flour

juice of ½ lemon

1 teaspoon ground cinnamon

½ teaspoon ground allspice

1 teaspoon vanilla extract

In a large bowl, toss together all the ingredients. Fill pie crusts with the apple filling and bake as instructed.

PECAN TARTS

Most pecan pies are sugar-and-fat bombs that can ring in at an outrageous 500 calories a slice. These are much less dangerous to your waistline and blood sugar, yet are everything you want out of a slice of pecan pie: buttery richness with tempered sweetness. The nutty butter scent that fills the house while they bake will evoke vivid dreams of autumn days.   *Serves 5   V, F*

Crust:

¾ cup pecans

1¼ cups whole wheat pastry flour

¼ cup coconut palm sugar or other granulated sugar

1 large egg

¼ cup (½ stick) cold unsalted butter, diced

1 teaspoon vanilla extract

Filling:

¾ cup pecans, coarsely chopped

⅓ cup dried currants

1 large egg

⅓ cup coconut palm sugar or brown sugar

3 tablespoons pure maple syrup

1 teaspoon pure vanilla extract

2 tablespoons unsalted butter, melted

½ teaspoon ground cinnamon

½ teaspoon ground ginger

¼ teaspoon salt

For the Crust: Place the pecans in the bowl of a food processor and pulse into small bits. Add the flour, sugar, egg, butter, and vanilla extract. Process until the mixture clumps together. Refrigerate for 30 minutes.

Preheat the oven to 350°F. Divide the pecan dough into 10 equal balls and place each in a medium muffin cup. Press the crusts down and up the sides of the muffin cups nearly all the way to the top.

For the Filling: Stir together all of the filling ingredients in a large bowl. Divide the mixture evenly among the crust cups. Bake until the edges of the crust begin to darken and become crispy, about 15 minutes. Let cool for several minutes before unmolding.

Top: PECAN TARTS, *page 132*
Bottom: BAKLAVA CUPS, *page 134*

BAKLAVA CUPS

When I think of baklava, what immediately comes to mind is a bike trip I took to Syria a few years back. Crisp and flaky on the outside with a sweet chewy middle, these are my tribute to one of the world's great desserts.
Serves 12   V

⅓ cup unsalted butter, melted, divided

½ cup coarsely chopped pecans

½ cup coarsely chopped shelled unsalted pistachios

⅓ cup chopped dried apricots

3 tablespoons plain bread crumbs

½ teaspoon ground cinnamon

½ teaspoon ground ginger (optional)

¼ teaspoon ground nutmeg

⅓ cup honey, plus more for serving

2 tablespoons coconut palm sugar or other granulated sugar

1 teaspoon grated lemon or orange zest

6 sheets phyllo dough, thawed

Preheat the oven to 350°F. Grease 12 medium muffin cups with some of the melted butter. In a large bowl, stir together the pecans, pistachios, apricots, bread crumbs, cinnamon, ginger, if using, nutmeg, 3 tablespoons of the melted butter, honey, sugar, and lemon or orange zest.

Very carefully place one sheet of phyllo on a flat work surface and cover the remaining sheets with a damp clean kitchen towel to keep them moist. Using a pastry brush, cover the surface with some of the remaining butter. Cover the first sheet with a second sheet of phyllo and brush with melted butter. Repeat until you have a stack of 3 layers. With the tip of a sharp knife or a pizza cutter, carefully cut the layered sheets into 3 segments from top to bottom and then slice from left to right at the midway point to make 6 total squares. Tuck the phyllo pastry squares into 6 medium muffin cups so that the bottoms are flat. Fill each phyllo cup with about 1½ tablespoons of the nut mixture. Gather up the 4 sides of each phyllo cup and seal together to form sachets. Brush the tops with some of the butter. Repeat with the remaining phyllo pastry and nut mixture.

Bake until the edges of the phyllo are golden, about 18 minutes. Let cool for several minutes before unmolding. Serve with additional honey drizzled on top.

STRAWBERRY YOGURT TARTS

Greek yogurt is perfect for healthy tarts because the liquid whey is already strained away, allowing it to set easily during baking. If you don't use Greek yogurt, you'll need to strain the yogurt through cheesecloth for at least two hours to thicken it. If needed, select oats such as Bob's Red Mill brand that are labeled "gluten-free." *Serves 12   V, G*

Crust:

1¼ cups quick-cook rolled oats (not instant)

¾ cup walnuts

¼ cup hemp seeds (optional)

2 tablespoons honey

1 large egg

¼ cup (½ stick) cold unsalted butter, diced

Filling:

1 cup plain low-fat or whole milk Greek yogurt

1 cup diced strawberries

2 tablespoons honey

2 teaspoons vanilla extract

1 teaspoon grated orange zest

sliced strawberries, for garnish

For the Crust: To make the crust, place the oats, walnuts, and hemp seeds, if using, in a food processor and pulse into small bits. Add the honey, egg, and butter. Process until the mixture clumps together. Refrigerate for 30 minutes.

Preheat the oven to 350°F. Divide the oat dough into 12 equal balls and place each in a medium muffin cup. Press the crusts down and up the sides of the muffin cups nearly all the way to the tops.

For the Filling: Stir together the yogurt, strawberries, honey, vanilla extract, and orange zest in a large bowl. Divide the yogurt mixture evenly among the crust cups. Bake until the edges of the crust begin to darken and yogurt has set, about 15 minutes. Let cool for several minutes before unmolding. The easiest way to unmold the tarts is to slide a butter knife between the crust and the tin and pop them out. Garnish with sliced strawberries, if desired.

ORANGE PANNA COTTA WITH JAVA-FIG COMPOTE

This elegant Italian dessert is usually made in ramekins with generous amounts of sugar and cream (the loose translation of "panna cotta" is "cooked cream"). Muffin tins are a great stand-in for ramekins and the combination of milk and creamy Greek yogurt helps sack some of the fat calories. *Serves 10   V, G*

Panna Cotta:

1 (1-tablespoon) packet gelatin

½ cup orange juice (from about 1 medium orange)

1⅓ cups low-fat milk or unflavored hemp milk

3 tablespoons light-colored natural cane sugar

⅔ cup plain low-fat or whole milk Greek yogurt

1 teaspoon grated orange zest

1 teaspoon vanilla extract

Compote:

1¼ cups strongly brewed coffee

20 dried Mission figs, stems trimmed and quartered (about 1 cup)

¼ cup honey

1 whole star anise

¼ teaspoon ground cinnamon

1 teaspoon grated lemon zest

For the Panna Cotta: In a small bowl, dissolve the gelatin in the orange juice and let sit for 10 minutes. In a medium saucepan over medium heat, bring the milk to a slight simmer. Add the sugar and stir to dissolve. Whisk in the gelatin-orange juice, yogurt, orange zest, and vanilla extract. Divide the mixture evenly among 10 medium muffin cups. Refrigerate until set, at least 4 hours. To unmold, run a butter knife around edges and invert the pan onto a plate.

For the Compote: In a medium saucepan, combine the coffee, figs, honey, star anise, cinnamon, and lemon zest. Bring to a boil over high heat, reduce heat the heat to low, and simmer, covered, for 20 minutes. With a slotted spoon, remove the figs and star anise from the pan. Simmer the liquid, uncovered, over medium-high heat until reduced and syrupy, 3 to 4 minutes. Return the figs to the pan; discard the star anise. Let cool before serving over the panna cottas.

Top: ORANGE PANNA COTTA WITH JAVA-FIG COMPOTE, *page 136*
Bottom: POMEGRANATE FRUIT SALAD, *page 138*

POMEGRANATE FRUIT SALAD

For a treat better than Jell-O, use your muffin cups to mold fruits and juices with gelatin for a lower-calorie, fresh-tasting dessert. I recommend using a silicone muffin tray, as you'll appreciate its flexibility when it comes to unmolding. Agar agar, a gelatinous substance derived from algae, is a vegan substitute for gelatin. Use 1 teaspoon agar agar for 2 cups liquid. It will set at room temperature.   *Serves 6*   G

1½ cups pomegranate juice, divided

1½ packets (1½ tablespoons) gelatin

½ cup water

½ cup green or red grapes, sliced in half

½ cup blueberries

½ cup raspberries

Place ¼ cup plus 2 tablespoons of the pomegranate juice in a large heatproof bowl and sprinkle the gelatin over the top. Let sit for 5 minutes. Place another ¼ cup plus 2 tablespoons of the pomegranate juice in a small saucepan and bring to a boil over medium-high heat. Add the hot pomegranate juice along with the remaining ¾ cups pomegranate juice and the water to the gelatin mixture. Whisk constantly until the gelatin has fully dissolved, about 1 minute. Divide the grapes, blueberries, and raspberries among 10 medium silicone muffin cups and pour the pomegranate mixture over the top. Refrigerate until set, about 4 hours.

To unmold the set gelatin, use a butter knife to loosen the edges, then dip the bottom of the muffin pan in warm water for about 10 seconds to loosen and carefully invert the muffin pan onto a tray. You may need to gently squeeze or tap the bottom of the silicone muffin cups slightly to help with unmolding.

ALMOND-CHERRY CLAFOUTIS

The quintessential French grandmotherly custardlike dessert, clafoutis hails from the Limousin region of France and is remarkably simple to put together. Just whiz together your batter in a blender and pour over the fruit. The tender batter swells around the cherries as it bakes in the oven. This version is gluten-free thanks the substitution of marvelous almond flour for white flour.   *Serves 12   V, G*

1½ cups pitted cherries, sliced in half

4 large eggs

3 tablespoons melted coconut oil or melted butter, cooled

1 teaspoon vanilla extract

½ teaspoon almond extract

⅓ cup honey

1 cup light coconut milk

½ teaspoon salt

½ teaspoon ground cinnamon

½ teaspoon ground ginger

¾ cup almond flour

confectioners' sugar (optional)

Preheat the oven to 350°F. Divide cherries among 12 medium muffin cups. Combine the eggs, coconut oil or butter, vanilla extract, almond extract, honey, coconut milk, salt, cinnamon, and ginger in a blender. Blend for a few seconds to mix the ingredients, add the almond flour, and blend until smooth.

Pour the almond mixture over the berries in the muffin cups and bake until golden and an inserted toothpick comes out clean. Let cool for several minutes before unmolding. Serve with a dusting of confectioners' sugar, if desired.

PISTACHIO BUTTER–DARK CHOCOLATE CUPS

If Reese's peanut butter cups are one of the most desirable corner store treats, what would a DIY version stuffed with pistachio butter, spiked with chile, and adorned with a whisper of fleur de sel be? One word: awesome! You can skip the step of skinning the pistachios before grinding, but the centers of the cups won't be as bright green. Use leftover pistachio butter as you would its peanut brethren on toast, crackers, or another batch of these gems.   *Serves 12   V, G, F*

½ cup shelled unsalted pistachios

2 tablespoons extra-virgin olive oil

¼ cup confectioners' sugar

14 ounces semisweet or bittersweet dark chocolate, chopped

¼ teaspoon chili powder or cayenne pepper

½ teaspoon fleur de sel

Bring a small pot of water to a boil. Add the pistachios and boil for 5 minutes. Drain and rinse under cold water. Working in batches, place the pistachios on a clean kitchen towel, fold, and rub off the skins. In a small dry skillet over medium heat, toast the pistachios until fragrant, about 4 minutes. Let cool.

Place the pistachios and olive oil in a food processor or high-powered blender and grind until smooth and buttery. Wipe down the sides as needed.

Line 24 mini muffin cups with paper liners. Melt the chocolate in a double boiler or a heatproof bowl placed over a saucepan of lightly simmering water, stirring regularly. Or, microwave the chocolate in a large microwave-safe bowl in 25-second increments on high power, stirring after each interval until melted. Stir in the chili powder or cayenne pepper. Drop 2 teaspoons of melted chocolate in each of the prepared muffin cups. Place 1 teaspoon pistachio butter on top followed by another 2 teaspoons melted chocolate. Sprinkle fleur de sel on top. Freeze until set, about 2 hours.

Top: PISTACHIO BUTTER—DARK CHOCOLATE CUPS, *page 140*
Bottom: RASPBERRY SEMIFREDDO WITH PECAN CRUST, *page 142*

RASPBERRY SEMIFREDDO WITH PECAN CRUST

For those of us that don't own an ice cream maker, Italian semifreddo, literally meaning "partially frozen," is a delicate, ice cream—like creamy treat within grasp. Its wonderful texture is achieved by incorporating air into the raspberry-cream mixture.   *Serves 12   V, F*

1 cup graham cracker crumbs

⅔ cup pecans, very finely chopped

½ cup pure maple syrup

3 cups fresh or thawed frozen raspberries

¼ cup coconut palm sugar or other granulated sugar

1 teaspoon vanilla extract

1 cup cold whipping cream

shaved dark chocolate, to serve

Line 12 medium muffin cups with paper liners. In a medium bowl, stir together the graham cracker crumbs, pecans, and maple syrup until everything is moist. Divide the mixture among the prepared muffin cups and press down to flatten contents.

Combine the raspberries, sugar, and vanilla extract in the bowl of a food processor or blender container and puree. Pour the puree into a large bowl. Whip the cream in a second large cold bowl using a cold whisk or electric mixer on medium speed just until soft peaks form. Fold the cream into the puree using a rubber spatula, working from the bottom of the bowl, until there are no signs of the cream. Pour the mixture into the muffin cups and level the tops. Cover with plastic wrap or aluminum foil and freeze until firm, at least 4 hours.

Unmold and place in a zip-top bag for storage in the freezer. When ready to serve, let sit at room temperature for about 20 minutes to soften, and top with shaved dark chocolate, if desired.

FROZEN RASPBERRY-LEMON MUFFINS

Having ready-to-bake homemade muffins in your freezer is so convenient for those times when you have a muffin craving but lack the time or energy to make them from scratch.   *Serves 12   V, F*

2 cups whole wheat pastry flour

1 teaspoon baking powder

½ teaspoon baking soda

½ teaspoon ground ginger

½ teaspoon salt

2 large eggs

⅔ cup buttermilk

⅓ cup melted coconut oil or other oil

⅔ cup coconut palm sugar or other granulated sugar

1 teaspoon grated lemon zest

2 tablespoons lemon juice

1 teaspoon vanilla extract

1 cup fresh or frozen raspberries, plus more for topping

In a large bowl, stir together the flour, baking powder, baking soda, ginger, and salt. In a second large bowl, lightly beat the eggs. Whisk in the buttermilk, oil, sugar, lemon zest, lemon juice, and vanilla extract. Add the dry ingredients to the wet ingredients and stir gently to combine. Fold in the raspberries.

Divide the mixture among 12 medium muffin cups, place 3 raspberries on top of each, and freeze until solid, about 3 hours. Unmold and transfer the frozen muffin batters to a zip-top bag until ready to bake.

When ready to bake, preheat the oven to 350°F. Place the muffins back into the muffin cups and bake until an inserted toothpick comes out clean, about 30 minutes. Let cool for several minutes before unmolding.

SOUR CHERRY—MINT POPS

As a lover of all things sour, whenever local fresh tart cherries are in season and available at our farmers' market, I grab them. They really make these pops, well, pop in your mouth. Packaged pitted frozen cherries can also be used for this recipe.   *Serves 12*   V, G, F

1½ cups water

¼ cup fresh mint, packed

¼ cup coconut palm sugar or other granulated sugar

1½ cups pitted sour cherries

juice of ½ lemon

In a small saucepan over high heat, bring the water to a simmer. Turn off the heat, add the mint, and let steep for 15 minutes. With a slotted spoon, remove the mint from the pan and discard. Add the sugar to the water and heat over medium-low heat until dissolved, stirring regularly.

Place the sweetened mint water, cherries, and lemon juice in a blender and puree until the cherries have broken down. Divide the mixture among 24 mini muffin cups or 12 medium muffin cups and cover with a sheet of foil. Using a sharp knife, make small slits in the foil in the middle of each filled muffin cup and slide in a Popsicle or coffee stirring stick. (The foil holds the sticks in place as the mixture freezes). Freeze until solid, about 4 hours.

Unmold the pops and place in a zip-top bag for storage in the freezer. If you have trouble unmolding the frozen cups, try placing the bottom of the muffin tray in warm water for several seconds, being careful not to thaw the pops.

Top: SOUR CHERRY—MINT POPS, *page 144*
Bottom: FROZEN BERRIES WITH WHITE CHOCOLATE CASHEW CREAM, *page 146*

FROZEN BERRIES WITH WHITE CHOCOLATE CASHEW CREAM

Ripe berries are one of the gastronomic highlights of summer, and I can't think of a better use for them than this luscious treat. The berry combination below is just a guideline. Use any mixture you desire based on what's in season. I enjoy eating these straight out of the freezer, but you can also let them soften at room temperature for several minutes. Betchya you can't eat just one!   *Serves 12*   *V, G, F*

1 cup unsalted raw cashews

6 ounces high-quality white chocolate, chopped

1 teaspoon vanilla extract

½ cup fresh blueberries

½ cup fresh currants

½ cup fresh raspberries

To make cashew cream, place the cashews in a bowl, cover with water, and soak for at least 2 hours. Drain and place in a blender along with barely enough fresh water to cover the nuts. Blend until smooth, 1 to 2 minutes.

To make the chocolate mixture, heat the cashew cream, white chocolate, and vanilla extract in small saucepan over low heat, stirring regularly, until the chocolate has melted. Line 12 medium muffin cups with paper liners, and divide the blueberries, currants, and raspberries among the cups. Pour the chocolate mixture evenly over the berries and freeze until solid, about 4 hours.

Unmold the chocolate-berry cups and place in a zip-top bag for storage in the freezer until ready to serve.

YOGURT-CANTALOUPE POPS

Who needs Popsicle molds when you have a trusty muffin tin? These are a great way to satisfy sweet cravings without wrecking your waistline. The combination of Greek yogurt, basil, and cantaloupe with a whisper of honey hits all the right notes: sweet, creamy, fresh. Gorgeous.

Serves 12   V, G, F

1 medium cantaloupe

1 cup plain or vanilla low-fat Greek yogurt

⅓ cup water

2 tablespoons honey

¼ cup finely chopped fresh basil

juice of 1 lime

Scoop out the flesh of the cantaloupe, discarding the seeds, and place in a blender along with the remaining ingredients. Process until well combined. Add more water if the mixture is too thick.

Divide the mixture among 24 mini muffin cups or 12 medium muffin cups and cover with a sheet of foil. Using a sharp knife, make small slits in the foil in the middle of each filled muffin cup and slide in a Popsicle or coffee stirring stick. (The foil holds the sticks in place as the mixture freezes). Freeze until solid, about 4 hours.

Unmold the popsicles and place in a zip-top bag for storage in the freezer. If you have trouble unmolding the frozen cups, try placing the bottom of the muffin tray in warm water for several seconds, being careful not to thaw the pops.

CAPPUCCINO CUPS

Coffee-spiked ice cream, chocolate, and pecans—oh, my. You can purchase chocolate wafers and crush them into very small bits in a food processor or by placing them in a zip-top bag and using a rolling pin. Chocolate crumbs are also available in the baking supply section of most supermarkets. The cappuccino-coconut ice-cream from Coconut Bliss is outstanding, but you can use your preferred brand. Make sure to use paper liners for these. *Serves 12   V, F*

1 cup chocolate cookie crumbs

2 tablespoons unsalted butter, melted, or melted coconut oil

1 pint cappuccino-flavored coconut or dairy ice-cream, slightly softened

2 ounces dark chocolate, chopped into chunks

⅓ cup chopped pecans

1 teaspoon vanilla extract

½ teaspoon ground cinnamon

¼ teaspoon ground nutmeg

2 tablespoons cocoa nibs (optional)

Line 12 medium muffin cups with paper liners. In a medium bowl, stir together the chocolate crumbs and butter. Divide the mixture the prepared muffin cups. Press down to compact the contents.

In a second medium bowl, stir together the ice cream, dark chocolate, pecans, vanilla extract, cinnamon, and nutmeg. Spoon the mixture into the muffin cups on top of the crumb crust. Sprinkle the tops with cocoa nibs, if using. Freeze until solid, about 3 hours. Unmold the cappuccino cups (leaving the paper liners on) and store in a zip-top bag in the freezer.

RESOURCES

Gear

Pampered Chef (www.pamperedchef.com)
Stoneware and well-performing mini muffin tins.

Demarle at Home (www.demarleathome.com)
Makers of the outstanding Flexipan muffin trays. Bid adieu to stressful unmolding.

PaperChef (www.paperchef.com)
Non-stick muffin cup parchment paper liners.

Wilton (www.wilton.com)
An assortment of silicone and sturdy metal muffin tins.

Foods

Bob's Red Mill (www.bobsredmill.com)
A dizzying array of dried beans, flours, and grains. Bob, you rock!

California Olive Ranch (www.californiaoliveranch.com)
Gourmet-tasting olive oil without the hefty price tag.

Eden Organic (www.edenfoods.com)
A good source for organic canned items such as beans packed in BPA-free cans.

Lundberg Family Farms (www.lundberg.com)
Delicious whole-grain rice varieties, gluten-free pasta, and brown rice syrup.

Manitoba Harvest (www.manitobaharvest.com)
Forward-thinking company supplying hemp foods such hemp seeds, hemp milk, and hemp protein powders.

MatchaSource (www.matchasource.com)

Your best bet for superior matcha green tea powder. I'm particularly fond of the Gotcha Matcha. A splurge never tasted so good.

Navitas Naturals (www.navitasnaturals.com)

A stunning offering of unique foods, including coconut palm sugar, raw cocoa powder, cocoa nibs, and a variety of superfruit powders such as acai. I think they should hire me to scout for products in exotic locales.

Nutiva (www.nutiva.com)

One of the best coconut oils around. They also carry hemp seeds and oil, chia seeds, and more.

Royal Hawaiian Honey (www.royalhawaiianhoney.com)

Local honey is always a smart buy, but these tasty honeys are so temptingly good you'll want to keep a jar on hand.

Sun-Maid (www.sunmaid.com)

Plenty of dried fruit options that are consistently good quality.

Nielsen-Massey Vanillas (www.nielsenmassey.com)

Top-notch vanilla, almond, and other flavoring extracts.

Wild Planet (www.wildplanetfoods.com)

A selection of sustainably caught canned seafood packaged in BPA-free tins. Try them and you'll never go back to the mass-marketed stuff.

Zico (www.zico.com)

Ultra-refreshing coconut water. Their chocolate flavor is particularly brag worthy.

Conversions

MEASURE	EQUIVALENT	METRIC
1 teaspoon	--	5 milliliters
1 tablespoon	3 teaspoons	14.8 milliliters
1 cup	16 tablespoons	236.8 milliliters
1 pint	2 cups	473.6 milliliters
1 quart	4 cups	947.2 milliliters
1 liter	4 cups + 3½ tablespoons	1000 milliliters
1 ounce (dry)	2 tablespoons	28.35 grams
1 pound	16 ounces	453.49 grams
2.21 pounds	35.3 ounces	1 kilogram
325°F/350°F/375°F/400°F	--	165°C/177°C/190°C/200°C

RECIPE INDEX

Acknowledgments

There was no shortage of individuals who contributed to this book in one way or another. Thank you to the real farmers at the St. Jacob's Farmers' Market for continuing to grow and sell real food despite a food system that continues to be up against you. Thank you to Mickey McGuire of Mickey McGuire's Cheese for always proving that high-quality cheese is not fungible with mass-produced impostors. My taste buds thank the representatives of the companies mentioned in the resource section. To our neighbor Kristijana Rakic, a big high-five for having the willing palate to try out many of the recipes that adorn this book. Thank you Kelly Reed at Ulysses Press for having the confidence that I could succeed at completing my first cookbook. Joan and John Macarthur, your unwavering support from my humble beginnings as an unsatisfied personal trainer to a busy recipe developer and writer is something I cherish greatly. Though we no longer see each other as much we should, to Mom, Dad, and brother, Glen, I can't express enough how much my professional success is tied to your loving nourishment over the years.

Most importantly, I can't thank enough my partner and recipe guinea pig Tabi Ferguson. Working on this book while maintaining a busy writing career at times seemed like a Sisyphean effort, turning me into a grumpy companion at the dinner table. You stood by me with great compassion during my lowliest moments, and for that, I have never loved you more.

About the Author

MATT KADEY is a registered dietitian, freelance nutrition writer, recipe developer, and travel photographer based in Waterloo, Ontario, Canada. As a prolific magazine writer, his nutrition, recipe, and travel articles have appeared in dozens of prestigious publications, including *Men's Health*, *Alive*, *Women's Health*, *Shape*, *Prevention*, *Eating Well*, *Men's Journal*, *Vegetarian Times*, *Runner's World*, *Bicycling*, and *Fit Pregnancy*. As an avid cyclist, Matt has cycled and feasted his way through numerous countries, including Sri Lanka, New Zealand, Laos, Thailand, Cuba, Cambodia, Ireland, Ethiopia, Belize, and Jordan. He is also a former provincial mountain bike champion in his age category. You can find Matt at mattkadey.com or www.muffintinmania.com where he continues his infatuation with the muffin tin.